COMMUNITY POWER AND DECISION-MAKING:

An International Handbook

by

IRVING P. LEIF

The Scarecrow Press, Inc.
Metuchen, N.J.   1974

Library of Congress Cataloging in Publication Data

Leif, Irving P   1947-
    Community power and decision-making.

    1. Community power—Bibliography. 2. Decision
-making—Bibliography. 3. Power (Social sciences)—
Bibliography. I. Title.
Z7164.C842L43   016.30115'5   74-4171
ISBN 0-8108-0717-3

TABLE OF CONTENTS

iii

1-1

INTRODUCTION

Community power and decision-making have been widely researched over the past twenty years by sociologists and political scientists. The resulting literature has been massive. This handbook attempts to bring together all this research in a useful reference format for scholars.

This handbook differs from other reference works in the area in several ways. First, it is international in scope. The handbook includes research on community power and decision-making in English as well as other languages. Since comparative studies are becoming increasingly important, this aspect of the handbook will provide scholars with new materials that they might not have been aware of because of language barriers or the unavailability of non-American journals.

Second, this handbook attempts to be completely comprehensive. It includes books, journal articles, doctoral dissertations, masters' theses, and papers presented at scholarly meetings. In some cases this means duplication. For instance, a paper presented at a scholarly meeting is many times later published. Often, however, it is edited to meet the specifications and space limitations of the journal or book in which it is to appear. This means that useful information may be left out of the published version. So, both the original version and the published version are listed herein in case the scholar desires to check the original version of the paper.

While this handbook aims at total inclusiveness, naturally some obstacle or another has prevented all research from being listed. For one thing, there is no central listing of masters' theses; so, only those theses that I am aware of through personal contacts or that have been footnoted in published works have been listed.

It is hoped that this handbook will become a useful research tool for all scholars in the area of community power and decision-making.

Acknowledgments

Through the course of compiling this handbook, I have received good advice and suggestions from many scholars. It was often their clues that led me to certain research I had not previously been aware of. Their names are too numerous to mention.

The original idea to compile a bibliography for my own personal research purposes came from Leonard U. Blumberg. From his suggestion, I compiled a bibliography and soon realized that it had gone beyond its original intent and was then more comprehensive than other published bibliographies. From that original bibliography evolved this handbook.

Parts of this handbook originally appeared in a work in the Current Sociology series jointly sponsored by UNESCO and the International Sociological Association. I would like to thank them for permission to reprint some of my work from that volume.

Also, I would like to thank my co-author on that project, Terry N. Clark, for his help and advice on this handbook over the years. He provided me with valuable information on the non-American literature as well as providing suggestions on some of the annotations.

Finally, over the years, secretarial and editorial assistance has been very adequately provided by Pamela S. Bracken, Diane Sears, and Margie Hoagland.

COMMUNITY POWER THEORY

POWER

1 Abramson, E., H. A. Cutler, R. W. Kautz, and M. Men-
   delson. 1958. "Social Power and Commitment
   Theory." American Sociological Review 23 (February): 15-22.
   Power is defined by the combination of actors, the
   lines of action open to them, and the commitments
   they have to society.

2 Agger, Robert. 1956. "Power Attributions in the Local Community: Theoretical and Research Considerations." Social Forces 34 (May): 322-331.
   A study of the attribution of power by selected
   community residents and their nominations. A
   mapping of the power structure did reveal that there
   was a small group who were attributed to hold power
   in the community.

3 Anton, Thomas. 1963. "Power, Pluralism and Local
   Politics." Administrative Science Quarterly 7 (March):
   425-458.
   An examination and critique of the pluralist positions on the study of local community power.

4 _____. 1963. "Rejoinder to Robert Dahl's Critique
   of 'Power, Pluralism, and Local Politics'." Administrative Science Quarterly 8 (September): 257-268.

5 Bachrach, Peter. 1962. Elite Consensus and Democracy." Journal of Politics 24 (August): 439-452.
   A critique of the democratic elite theories of
   Truman, Mills and Berle. Bachrach argues against
   elite consensus and for popular consensus on the
   important issues of the day.

6   _____, and Morton Baratz. 1962. "Two Faces of Power." American Political Science Review 56 (December): 947-952.

Bachrach and Baratz argue that both elitists and pluralists have only studied one face of power; that of decisions that actually took place. Past studies have failed to study those issues which have not been raised in the community because of their possible extremism. In other words, non-decisions must be studied to find out who was responsible for the suppression of them as a dimension of power and influence.

7   Barkley, Raymond. 1955. "Theory of the Elite and the Mythology of Power." Science and Society 19 (Spring): 97-106.

Barkley argues that universal democracy is possible through the active participation of the population as a whole.

8   Bauman, Z. 1962. "O Pojeciu Wladzy" [The Concept of Power]. Studia Socjologiczno Polityczne 13: 7-27.

Power can be likened to the concept of influence. Political power is defined as actors acting within the area of conflicts of classes. Power can be viewed as a factor in domination or as one element in the decision-making process.

9   Bensman, Joseph, and Arthur Vidich. 1962. "Power Cliques in Bureaucratic Society." Social Research 29 (Winter): 467-474.

Bensman and Vidich define power in terms of power cliques. These power cliques are defined as inter-institutional and occur at all levels of decision-making.

10   Bernard, Stephane. 1967. "Potere e Influenza: Contributo allo Studio del Sistema Politico" [Power and Influence: A Contribution to the Study of Political Systems]. Tempi Moderni 10 (Spring); 99-113.

11   Bierstedt, Robert. 1950. "An Analysis of Social Power." American Sociological Review 15 (December): 730-738.

An examination of the concept of social power. Power is defined as a social phenomenon and is distinguished from prestige, influence, dominance, rights, force and authority. Power is defined as

latent force and authority is defined as institutional
power. The sources of power reside in a combination of numbers, social organization and economic
resources.

12 Bonjean, Charles M. 1964. "Class, Status, and Power
Reputation." Sociology and Social Research 49 (October): 69-75.
Bonjean found that there was a relationship between
stratification components and methodological types of
community leaders (symbolic, visible, and concealed).
Persons who received a high status ranking also were
perceived as possessing power.

13 Burtenshaw, Claude J. 1968. "The Political Theory of
Pluralist Democracy." Western Political Quarterly
21 (December): 577-587.

14 Butler, Jay. 1960. "On Power and Authority: An Exchange on Concept." American Sociological Review
25 (October): 731-732.
Butler posits power as a superordinate concept to
authority and influence. Authority and influence become subsystems under power.

15 Cartwright, Dorwin. 1959. "A Field Theoretical Conception of Power." In Studies in Social Power,
edited by Dorwin Cartwright. Ann Arbor, Michigan:
Institute for Social Research, University of Michigan.
183-220.

16 _____, editor. 1959. Studies in Social Power.
Ann Arbor, Mich.: Institute for Social Research,
University of Michigan.

17 Champlin, John R. 1970. "On the Study of Power."
Politics and Society 1 (November): 91-111.

18 _____. 1971. Power. New York: Atherton
Press.

19 Chazel, F. 1964. "Reflexions sur la Conception Par-
sonienne du Pouvoir et de l'Influence" [Reflections on
the Parsonsian Concept of Power and Influence].
Revue Française de Sociologie 5 (Oct.-Dec.): 387-
401.

20 Clark, Terry N. 1967. "The Concept of Power: Some
    Overemphasized and Underrecognized Dimensions:
    An Examination with Special Reference to the Local
    Community." Southwestern Social Science Quarterly
    48 (December): 271-286.

21 _____. 1968. "Social Stratification, Differentiation
    and Integration." In Community Structure and Deci-
    sion-Making: Comparative Analyses, edited by Terry
    N. Clark. San Francisco: Chandler Pub. Co.
    25-44.

22 Cowgill, Donald O. 1964. "Power as a Process in an
    Urban Community." In Approaches to the Study of
    Urbanization, edited by Richard Stauber. Lawrence:
    University of Kansas Publications, Government Re-
    search Center Series, No. 27. 168-175.

23 Crespigny, A. 1968. "Power and Its Forms." Po-
    litical Studies 16 (June): 192-205.

24 Dahl, Robert. 1957. "The Concept of Power." Be-
    havioral Science 2 (July): 201-215.
        A discussion of the concept of power elaborating
    Dahl's basic definition of power; A has power over
    B to the extent that he can get B to do something
    that B would not otherwise do. One of Dahl's most
    important analytical discussions of the concept of
    power.

25 _____. 1958. "A Critique of the Ruling Elite
    Model." American Political Science Review 52
    (June): 463-469.
        A critique of the theses of Mills and Hunter is
    presented. Dahl argues that insufficient evidence
    was presented by either Mills or Hunter that a
    ruling elite exists in the nation or in a community.
    Dahl proposes a test to find out whether a ruling
    elite really exists: the analysis of a series of im-
    portant and concrete decisions where clear differences
    in preference distinguish the elite from the general
    citizenry. If the elite preferences prevail in such
    situations, only then can a ruling elite be said to
    exist.

26 _____. 1961. "Equality and Power in American
    Society." In Power and Democracy in America,

edited by William V. D'Antonio and Howard J. Ehrlich.
Notre Dame, Ind.: University of Notre Dame Press.
73-89.

27 _____. 1966. "Further Reflections on 'The Elitist
Theory of Democracy'." American Political Science
Review 60 (June): 296-305.
A critique of Jack L. Walker's essay on the elitist
theory of democracy. Dahl criticizes Walker on the
grounds of theory, selection of supporting data, and
Walker's criteria for the selection of normative writings which Dahl argues are really descriptive, empirical theories.

28 _____. 1955. "Hierarchy, Democracy, and Bargain-
320.7   ing in Politics and Economics." In Research Frontiers
R432r   in Politics and Government, by Stephen Bailey et al.
Washington, D.C.: Brookings Institution. 49-69.

29 _____. 1968. "Power." In The International Ency-
qr303   clopedia of the Social Sciences. New York: Macmillan
I61e   and The Free Press. Volume 12, 405-415.

30 _____. 1963. "Reply to Thomas Anton's 'Power,
Pluralism, and Local Politics'." Administrative
Science Quarterly 8 (September): 250-256.

31 Dahlstrom, Edmund. 1966. "Exchange, Influence and
Power." Acta Sociologica 9: 237-284.

32 D'Antonio, William V., and Howard J. Ehrlich. 1961.
"Democracy in America: Retrospect and Prospect."
321.8   In Power and Democracy in America, edited by
P887p   William V. D'Antonio and Howard J. Ehrlich. Notre
Dame, Ind.: University of Notre Dame Press. 125-
152.

33 Deutsch, Karl. 1967. "On the Concepts of Politics and
Power." Journal of International Affairs 21: 232-241.

34 Dusek, V. 1969. "Falsifiability and Power Elite
Theory." Journal of Comparative Administration 1
(August): 198-212.

35 Ehrlich, Howard J. 1961. "Power and Democracy: A
321.8   Critical Discussion." In Power and Democracy in
P887p   America, edited by William V. D'Antonio and Howard

J. Ehrlich.   Notre Dame, Ind.:   University of Notre Dame Press.   91-123.

36   Emerson, Richard M.   1962.   "Power-Dependence Relations."   American Sociological Review 27 (February): 31-41.
Power relationships are defined in terms of a reciprocal power-dependence relation and the properties of balance and "balancing operations" that occur in such relationships.

37   Engelmann, Hugo O.   1965.   "Power and Tension."   Journal of Human Relations 13:   155-166.

38   Evers, Hans-Dieter, editor.   1969.   Case Studies in Social Power.   Leiden, Netherlands: E. J. Brill.

39   Farneti, Paolo.   1969.   "Dimensioni del Potere Politico" [Dimensions of Political Power].   Quaderni di Sociologia 18 (Jul.-Sept.):   337-362.

40   French, J. R. P., Jr.   1956.   "A Formal Theory of Social Power."   Psychological Review 63 (May): 181-194.

41   _____, and Bertram Raven.   1959.   "The Bases of Social Power."   In Studies in Social Power, edited by Dorwin Cartwright.   Ann Arbor: Institute for Social Research, University of Michigan.   150-168.

42   Furuki, Tasiaki.   1967.   "The Pluralistic Power Theory and Local Politics."   Shakaigaku Hyoron 17 (January): 39-54.

43   Gamson, William A.   1968.   Power and Discontent.   Homewood, Ill.:   The Dorsey Press.
Power and discontent are viewed from the complementary perspectives of potential partisans and authorities.   Gamson sees binding decision-making as an important function of authorities.   His discussion also focuses on how authorities control potential partisans.

44   Garvey, G.   1970.   "The Domain of Politics."   Western Political Quarterly 23 (March):   120-137.
Garvey integrates recent economic theory with political theory.   He defines power as the ability to force the decision-maker to take options that he would not

necessarily consider for himself because they would have a negative utility for the decision-maker.

45   Gaudemet, J. 1962. "Esquisse d'une Sociologie Historique du Pouvoir" [Sketch of a Historical Sociology of Power]. Politique 19-20 (Jul.-Dec.): 195-234.
A review of the fundamental uses of the concept of power. Gaudemet views power as a reciprocal process and argues that the functioning of power revolves around three ideas: orders, constraint, and wealth.

46   Giddens, A. 1968. " 'Power' in the Recent Writings of Talcott Parsons." Sociology 2 (September): 257-272.

47   Gitlin, Todd. 1965. "Local Pluralism as Theory and Ideology." Studies on the Left 5: 21-45.

48   Goffman, I. W. 1957. "Status Consistency and Preference for Change in Power Distribution." American Sociological Review 22 (June): 275-281.
Goffman finds support for the hypothesis of an inverse relationship between degree of status consistency and the desire for a change in the distribution of power. This relationship was found to be related to the stratum position of the individual.

49   Goldhammer, Herbert, and Edward A. Shils. 1939. "Types of Power and Status." American Journal of Sociology 45 (September): 171-182.
Power is defined as the influencing of the behavior of others in accordance with the actor's own intentions. It is also distinguished by its legitimacy as recognized by the subordinate individuals.

50   Gravel, Pierre Bettez. 1969. "Diffuse Power as a Commodity: A Case Study From Gisaka." In Case Studies in Social Power, edited by Hans-Dieter Evers. Leiden, Netherlands: E. J. Brill. 3-16.

51   Holm, Kurt. 1969. "Zum Begriff der Macht" [On the Concept of Power]. Kölner Zeitschrift für Soziologie und Sozial-Psychologie 21 (June): 269-288.
A theoretical definition of power is formulated. Holm finds power to be dispositional, relative, and quantitative. Power exists if A has domination over B by possession of sufficient instruments to do so

or if B believes in the legitimacy of A's power.

52 Iribarne, Manuel Fraga. 1954. "El Poder como Con-
cepto Sociologico y como Base de la Politica" [Power
as a Sociological Concept and as the Basis of Politics].
Revista Internacional de Sociologia (Madrid) 12 (Oct. -
Dec.): 659-703.

53 James, B. J. 1964. "The Issue of 'Power'." Public
Administration Review 24 (March): 47-51.
        A review essay examining the concept of power by
various writers. James finds their works to be ster-
ile because of the relatively powerless nature of the
academic role.

54 Kariel, Henry. 1961. The Decline of American
Pluralism. Stanford, Cal. : Stanford University
Press.

55 Keynes, Edward, and David Ricci, editors. 1970. Political Power: Community and Democracy. Chicago:
Rand McNally.
        A collection of readings on power studies, method-
ological problems in power studies, and power studies
and democratic theory.

56 Kimberly, James C. , and Lynne G. Zucker. 1971.
"Relations Between Status and Power: Toward An
Integration of Contemporary Conceptions. " Unpub-
lished paper presented at the meeting of the Southern
Sociological Society.

57 Kimbrough, Ralph B. 1964. "Development of a Concept of Social Power. " In The Politics of Education
in the Local Community, edited by Robert S. Cahill
and Stephen Hencley. Danville, Ill. : The Interstate
Printers & Publishers. 93-110.

58 Kornberg, Allan, and Simon D. Perry. 1966. "Conceptual Models of Power and Their Applicability to
Empirical Research in Politics. " Political Science
(New Zealand) 18 (March): 52-70.
        Various conceptual models of power are examined.
Dahl, March, Simon, and Cartwright are examined
and compared. Kornberg and Perry do not believe
that any of these models has generated much research or been incorporated in any other theoretical
models.

59 Kornhauser, Arthur, editor. 1957. Problems of Power in American Democracy. Detroit: Wayne State University Press.

60 Lasswell, Harold, and Abraham Kaplan. 1950. Power and Society. New Haven: Yale University Press.
    A classic theoretical discussion of power and influence. Two fundamental concepts it helped encourage in later work were the scope of power and resources.

320.1
L348po

61 Lee, Kuo-wei. 1966. "Harold D. Lasswell's Theory of Power: Its Value as a Framework for Political Analysis." Unpublished Ph.D. dissertation, University of Oregon.
    Lee found that most researchers have modified Lasswell's concept of power before using it in their research. If Lasswell's concept is fully followed, the research should center on the interplay of power and the personalities of the power elite.

62 Lehman, E. W. 1969. "Toward a Macrosociology of Power." American Sociological Review 34 (August): 453-465.
    An examination of power as a property of macroscopic social systems. In a macroscopic social system, power is viewed as a generalized capacity, having multiple resource bases, holding the ability to convert symbolic capacity based on social attributes into normative resources, and the specialization of vertical intermember power networks.

63 McFarland, Andrew S. 1969. Power and Leadership in Pluralist Systems. Stanford, Cal.: Stanford University Press.

320.1
M143p

64 _____. 1967. "Power, Critical Decisions, and Leadership: An Analysis of Empirical Pluralist Theory." Unpublished Ph.D. dissertation, University of California, Berkeley.

65 McKee, James B. 1956. "The Power to Decide." In Society and Man, edited by Meyer Weinberg and Oscar Shabat. Englewood Cliffs, N.J.: Prentice-Hall. 39-70.

66 March, James G. 1966. "The Power of Power." In Varieties of Political Theory, edited by David Easton.

Englewood Cliffs, N. J.: Prentice-Hall. 39-70.

67   Marshall, T. H. 1969. "Reflections on Power."
     Sociology 3 (May): 141-155.

68   Martin, Roderick. 1971. "The Concept of Power: A
     Critical Defense." British Journal of Sociology 22
     (September): 240-257.

69   Merelman, Richard M. 1968. "On the Neo-Elitist
     Critique of Community Power." American Political
     Science Review 62 (June): 451-460.
         An investigation of the problem of non-decision-
     making. Merelman concludes that the pluralist pre-
     mises more accurately portray the community power
     structure since no elite can operate on the basis of
     non-decision-making alone.

70   Merriam, Charles. 1964. Political Power. New
     York: Collier.

71   Mileur, Jerome Maurice. 1971. "Pluralist Power and
     the American Science of Politics: An Immaculate
     Conception." Unpublished Ph. D. dissertation,
     Southern Illinois University.

72   Miller, Delbert C. 1968. "Power, Complementarity,
     and the Cutting Edge of Research." Sociological
     Focus 1 (Summer): 1-17.

73   Minogue, K. R. 1959. "Power in Politics." Political
     Studies 7 (October): 269-289.
         A social and political theory is presented which
     does not have power as its basis.

74   Moore, Barrington, 1958. "Notes on the Process of
     Acquiring Power." In Political Power and Social
     Theory, by Barrington Moore. Cambridge, Mass.:
     Harvard University Press. 1-29.

75   Morgenthau, Hans. 1958. "Power as a Political Con-
     cept." In Approaches to the Study of Politics, edited
     by Roland Young. Evanston, Ill.: Northwestern Uni-
     versity Press. 66-77.

76   Mott, Paul E. 1970. "Configurations of Power." In
     The Structure of Community Power, edited by

Michael Aiken and Paul Mott. New York: Random House. 85-100.

77 _____. 1970. "Power, Authority, and Influence."
In The Structure of Community Power, edited by
Michael Aiken and Paul Mott. New York: Random
House. 3-16.
Mott defines social control, authority, influence,
and power and discusses their interrelationships.

78 Nagel, Jack Henry. 1972. "The Descriptive Analysis
of Power." Unpublished Ph.D. dissertation, Yale
University.

79 _____. 1968. "Some Questions About the Concept
of Power." Behavioral Science 13 (March): 129-137.
A review of past definitions of power with special
attention to the theoretical definitions of Dahl and
Harsanyi.

80 Neumann, Franz. 1950. "Approaches to the Study of
Political Power." Political Science Quarterly 65
(June): 161-180.

81 Newton, Kenneth. 1969. "A Critique of the Pluralist
Model." Acta Sociologica 12: 209-223.
In comparing Hunter and Dahl, Newton argues that
their differences lie in what they had hoped to find.
The debate between the two is an ideological one.
America does not conform to the pluralist model that
Dahl thought it did.

82 Olson, David. 1967. "Comment by a Political Scientist." Southwestern Social Science Quarterly 48
(December): 292-296.
A response to Clark's paper on the concept of
power. Olson argues that there are five areas in
which additional empirical studies are needed. These
areas are external linkages into the community, non-
decisions, stages of issue development, measurement
of latent issues, and issue selection.

83 Oppenheim, Felix E. 1958. "An Analysis of Political
Control: Actual and Potential." Journal of Politics
20 (August): 515-534.
A theoretical discussion of power, influence, and
control.

84 _____. 1960. "Degrees of Power and Freedom."
    American Political Science Review 54 (June): 437-
    446.
        A theoretical discussion of power and freedom and
    the differences between them.

85 Padover, Saul. 1962. "Lasswell's Impact on the Study
    of Power in a Democracy." Social Research 29
    (Winter): 489-494.
        A review of the contributions of Harold Lasswell
    to the study of democracy and power. Lasswell's
    view of democracy is based on three notions: power,
    participation, and shared values. Politics is viewed
    by Lasswell as an irrational struggle for power.

86 Parenti, Michael. 1970. "Power and Pluralism: A
    View From the Bottom." Journal of Politics 32
    (August): 501-530.

87 Parsons, Talcott. 1963. "On the Concept of Influence."
    Public Opinion Quarterly 27 (Spring): 37-62.

88 _____. 1963. "On the Concept of Political Power."
    Proceedings of the American Philosophical Society
    107 (June): 232-262.

89 _____. 1957. "The Distribution of Power in Ameri-
    can Society." World Politics 10 (October): 123-143.
        A critique of Mills' The Power Elite. There is
    also a general discussion of the concept of power.

90 Partridge, P. H. 1963. "Some Notes on the Concept
    of Power." Political Studies 11 (June): 107-125.
        Partridge argues that researchers have not inves-
    tigated power correctly and have ignored certain as-
    pects of it. He does not feel that the concept of
    power is useful in explaining power structures.

91 Perrow, Charles. 1964. "The Sociological Perspective
    and Political Pluralism." Social Research 31 (Win-
    ter): 411-422.
        The sociological view of political pluralism was
    critiqued and found to suffer from several deficiencies.
    These deficiencies are the neglect of data on group
    membership, the neglect of the role of economic in-
    terests, and the minimization of the role of power in
    society.

92   Plessner, Helmuth. 1964. "The Emancipation of
        Power." Social Research 31 (Summer): 155-174.
            Plessner presented a formula for the intensification
        of the theoretical and practical problem of power.
        This need for an intensification has come about through
        the increasing influence of the state throughout society.

93   Polsby, Nelson. 1969. " 'Pluralism' in the Study of
        Community Power, or, Erklärung Before Verklärung
        in Wissenssoziologie." The American Sociologist 4
        (May): 118-122.
            Polsby seeks to correct the loose usage of the term
        pluralism. He offers three specific definitions, dis-
        tinguishing theory and method from substantive results.
        He criticizes the studies of Walton and Clark et al.
        concerning the relationship between discipline of the
        researcher, type of method, and substantive results.

94   Porket, Josef L. 1969. "Autouta--Moc--Vlio" [Author-
        ity--Power--Influence]. Sociologicky Casopis 5: 304-
        314.
            Power was defined as the possibility to evoke in-
        tended consequences while influence was defined as
        the possibility to evoke consequences.

95   Porsholt, L. 1970. "Om Begrepene 'Makt' og 'Innfly-
        telse' " [Some Remarks on 'Power' and 'Influence'].
        Internasjonal Politikk (Bergen) 3: 247-255.

96   Powers, Ronald C. "Power Actors and Social Change
        (Part 1)." Journal of Cooperative Extension 5 (Fall):
        153-163.
            The basic concepts of power and power structure
        are defined. The research on community power is
        reviewed with special attention given to that research
        which will affect extension work.

97   Raven, Bertram H. , and J. R. P. French, Jr. 1958.
        "Legitimate Power, Coercive Power and Observability
        in Social Influence." Sociometry 21 (June): 83-97.

98   Ricci, David. 1971. Community Power and Democratic
        Theory: The Logic of Political Analysis. New York:
        Random House.
            A collection of readings by the author and others
        on the theoretical perspectives that concern the re-
        searcher of community power.

99   Riker, William H.   1964.   "Some Ambiguities in the
       Notion of Power."   American Political Science Re-
       view 58 (June): 341-349.
          Riker argues that the ambiguities surrounding the
       concept power reflect ambiguities similarly found in
       the concept of causation.

100   Rogers, Mary Frances.   1972.   "A Theoretical Ap-
       proach to Community Power, Influence, and Decision-
       Making." Unpublished Ph. D. dissertation, Univer-
       sity of Massachusetts.

101   Rosenbaum, Allan.   1967.   "Community Power and
       Political Theory: A Case of Misrepresentation."
       Berkeley Journal of Sociology 12 (Summer): 91-116.
          A critique of the pluralist model with specific
       reference to the work of Nelson Polsby.

102   Schermerhorn, Richard A.   1961.   Society and Power.
       New York: Random House.

103   Segalman, R.   1966.   "An Interdisciplinary Approach
       to Power."   Rocky Mountain Social Science Journal
       3 (October): 9-15.

104   Simpson, Richard.   1967.   "Comment by a Sociologist."
       Southwestern Social Science Quarterly 48 (December):
       287-291.
          A comment on Clark's paper on the concept of
       power. After reviewing Clark's paper, Simpson
       makes several conclusions. First, more attention
       should be paid to the question of who benefits from
       governmental activities. Second, more attention
       should be paid to the causes of variation in commu-
       nity power arrangements. Third, the problem of
       how issues and groups differ from community to
       community should be examined.

105   Srauz-Hupe, Robert.   1956.   Power and Community.
       New York: Praeger.

106   Truman, D.   1953.   "Pluralism." In The Government
       Process, by D. Truman. New York: Knopf. 508-
       516.

107   Useem, John.   1950.   "The Sociology of Power." Un-
       published paper presented at the meeting of the

American Sociological Society.

108   Van Doorn, J. A. A.   1962-63.   "Sociology and the
      Problem of Power."   Sociologia Neerlandica 1 (Win-
      ter):   3-47.
            Power must be defined only in sociological terms.
      Power must also be acknowledged by those under its
      influence if social order is to be maintained.   Van
      Doorn sees three indices of power;   the exercise of
      power, social roles of power actors, and the social
      basis of power.

109   Walker, Jack L.   1966.   "A Critique of the Elitist
      Theory of Democracy."   American Political Science
      Review 60 (June):   285-295.
            A critique of the elite theory of democracy is pre-
      sented with special emphasis on shortcomings such
      as acceptance of the prevailing distribution of status
      in society and its inadequacy as a guide to empirical
      research.

110   _____.   1964.   "The Foundations of Democracy."
      American Journal of Economics and Sociology 23
      (January):   19-36.

111   Walter, Benjamin.   1964.   "On the Logical Analysis of
      Power-Attribution Procedures."   Journal of Politics
      26 (November):   850-866.
            Walter concludes that the findings of James March
      are still applicable.

112   Weber, Max.   1947.   "Power."   In The Theory of So-
      cial and Economic Organization, by Max Weber.
      New York: Oxford University Press.   152.
            Power is defined as the probability that an actor
      will be able to exert his will despite resistance from
      others.

113   Wrong, Dennis.   1968.   "Some Problems in Defining
      Social Power."   American Journal of Sociology 73
      (May):   673-681.
            A discussion of the concept of power especially
      dealing with the problems of defining actual and po-
      tential power.

LEADERSHIP

114   Banfield, Edward. 1958. "The Concept 'Leadership' in
      Community Research." Unpublished paper presented
      at the meeting of the American Political Science As-
      sociation.

115   Bell, Wendell, Richard Hill, and Charles Wright. 1961.
      Public Leadership. San Francisco: Chandler Pub.
      Co.

116   Browning, Rufus P., and Herbert Jacob. 1964. "Power
      Motivation and the Political Personality." Public
      Opinion Quarterly 28 (Spring): 75-90.

117   Clark, Terry N. 1969. "An Interchange Model of
      Community Leadership." Unpublished paper pre-
      sented at the Conference on Community Decision-
      Making, Milan, Italy.

118   _____. 1970. "A Model of Leadership and Policy
      Outputs." Washington, D.C.: Working Paper 705-
      70, The Urban Institute.

119   Dahl, Robert. 1960. "Leadership in a Fragmented
      Political System: Notes for a Theory." Unpublished
      paper presented at the Conference on Metropolitan
      Leadership, Northwestern University.

120   _____. 1959. "Patrician and Plebian." Unpublished
      paper presented at the meeting of the American So-
      ciological Association.

121   DiRenzo, Gordon J. 1967. "Professional Politicians
      and Personality Structures." American Journal of
      Sociology 73 (September): 217-225.
           The Rokeach Dogmatism Scale was administered
      to a group of Italian legislators. The professional
      politicians scored higher and were more dogmatic
      than non-politicians.

122   Downes, Bryan T. 1968. "Municipal Social Ranks and
      the Characteristics of Local Political Leaders."
      Midwest Journal of Political Science 12 (November):
      514-537.
           A study of the values and attitudes of suburban

councilmen and the relationship between municipal
social rank and the characteristics of councilmen.

123   Dye, Thomas.   1963.   "The Local-Cosmopolitan Dimen-
        sion and the Study of Urban Politics." Social Forces
        41 (March):   239-246.
             The local-cosmopolitan dimension is seen as re-
        lated to social stratification.   Higher status groups
        respond more to metropolitan problems.   Also, cos-
        mopolitans understand urban issues and urban poli-
        tics better than the locals.

124   Edwards, John.   1969.   "Organizational and Leadership
        Status." Sociological Inquiry 39 (Winter):   49-56.
             Edwards found that there were separate and in-
        dependent systems for communal ranking and asso-
        ciational ranking in regards to leader selection.

125   French, John R. P., Jr., and Richard Snyder.   1959.
        "Leadership and Interpersonal Power." In Studies
        in Social Power, edited by Dorwin Cartwright.   Ann
        Arbor: Institute for Social Research, University of
        Michigan.   118-149.

126   Friedrich, Carl J.   1961.   "Political Leadership and
        the Problem of the Charismatic Power." Journal
        of Politics 23 (February):   3-24.
             A theoretical analysis of the concept of charis-
        matic power.

127   George, Alexander L.   1968.   "Political Leadership
        and Social Change in American Cities." Daedalus
        94 (Fall):   1194-1217.

128   Gibb, Cecil.   1954.   "Leadership." In Handbook of
        Social Psychology, edited by Gardner Lindzey.
        Cambridge, Mass.:   Addison-Wesley.   Volume 2,
        877-920.

129   Holik, John S., and James H. Claycomb.   1964.
        "Search for Leadership." Journal of Cooperative
        Extension 2 (Winter):   235-241.

130   Jacob, Phillip E.   1970.   "The Demography of Develop-
        mental Leadership." Unpublished paper presented at
        the meeting of the International Sociological Associa-
        tion.

131   Jennings, M. Kent. 1963. "Public Administrators and
      Community Decision-Making." Administrative Science
      Quarterly 8 (June): 18-43.

132   Matthews, Donald R. 1954. Social Backgrounds of
      Political Decision-Makers. Garden City, N. Y. :
      Doubleday.

133   Merton, Robert. 1968. "Patterns of Influence: Local
      and Cosmopolitan Influentials." In Social Theory
      and Social Structure, by Robert Merton. New York:
      The Free Press. 441-474.

134   Naville, Pierre. 1963. "Technical Elites and Social
      Elites." Sociology of Education 37 (Fall): 27-29.

135   Nisbet, Robert. 1969. "The Twilight of Authority."
      The Public Interest 15 (Spring): 3-9.

136   Nix, Harold L. 1969. "Concepts of Community and
      Community Leadership." Sociology and Social Re-
      search 53 (July): 500-510.
           Nix argues that leaders can be classified along
      three dimensions: formal positions and formal func-
      tions, their scope of influence, and their basic or-
      ientation.

137   _____. 1968. "Concepts of Community and Commu-
      nity Leadership." Unpublished paper presented at
      the meeting of the Rural Sociological Society.

138   _____, Jennie McIntyre, and Charles J. Dudley.
      1967. "Bases of Leadership: The Cultural Ideal
      and Estimates of Reality." Southwestern Social
      Science Quarterly 48 (December): 423-432.
           The authors found that leaders in three cities
      agreed that there was a well defined culture of
      leadership. The leaders also agreed that there
      was a dissimilarity between ideal and actual quali-
      ties of leaders in this leadership culture. Finally,
      the cultural ideas was congruent with the value or-
      ientations of America in general.

139   Orbell, J. M. 1970. "An Information-Flow Theory of
      Community Influence." Journal of Politics 32 (May):
      322-338.
           Orbell found that actors with high involvement in

politics were likely to have a large amount of knowledge about local partisan politics. Actors with mod-
erate involvement conformed to the objective political
structure of their districts and actors with low involvement conformed to cues that they received from
the local district.

140 Parker, James H. 1968. "Moral Leadership in the
Community." Sociology and Social Research 53
(October): 88-94.
   A study of the selection of moral leaders in two
cities. Parker found that the general population
chose moral leaders that did not differ significantly
from general leaders. Professionals were chosen
as moral leaders more often than businessmen.

141 Parry, Geraint. 1969. Political Elites. New York:
Praeger.

142 Preston, James D. 1967. "A Typology of Community
Leadership." Unpublished Ph. D. dissertation,
Mississippi State University.

143 Rogers, Everett M. , and George M. Beal. 1958.
"The Importance of Personal Influence in the Adop-
tion of Technological Changes." Social Forces 36
(May): 329-335.

144 Ross, Murray G. , and Charles E. Hendry. 1957.
New Directions in Leadership. New York: Association Press.

145 Searing, Donald D. 1969. "Models and Images of Man
and Society in Leadership Theory." Journal of
Politics 31 (February): 3-31.
   An examination of the theoretical controversies
between elitists and pluralists concerning leadership.

146 Shoemaker, Donald J. , and Harold L. Nix. 1969.
"Community Influence: The Process of Becoming a
Community Leader. " Unpublished paper presented
at the meeting of the Southern Sociological Society.

147 Singh, Avtar. 1970. "A Reassessment of the Action
Approach to Community Leadership. " Sociologia
Ruralis 10: 3-20.
   Singh argues that community action participation

can be used as an adequate measure of community
leadership depending on the type of community
studied. Community development, values, and
physical isolation are key variables for understanding community leadership.

148 Smith, J. Vernon. 1970. "Community Leadership: A
     Paradigm for Research." Unpublished paper pre-
     sented at the meeting of the Rural Sociological So-
     ciety.

149 Smith, Lincoln. 1954. "Leadership in Local Govern-
     ment--The New England Town." Social Science 29
     (June): 147-154.

150 Sollie, Carlton R. 1961. "Community Leadership: A
     Critical Survey of the Literature and a Formulation
     of Hypotheses." Unpublished Master's thesis, Mis-
     sissippi State University.

151 Stemmler, J. 1954-54. "Führentypen" [Types of
     Leaders]. Kölner Zeitschrift für Soziologie 6: 187-
     217.

152 Ungern-Sternberg, R. von. 1959. "Uber die Begriffe
     'Führer' und 'Elite' " [On the Concepts of 'Leader'
     and 'Elite']. Schmollers Jahrbuch (Berlin) 79: 27-
     36.

DECISION-MAKING

153 Adrian, Charles R., and Charles Press. 1968. "De-
     cision Costs in Coalition Formation." American
     Political Science Review 62 (June): 556-563.
         To determine the costs of a winning coalition, at
     least eight decision costs must be summed; this
     yields the membership in the winning coalition.

154 Alford, Robert R. 1973. "Strategies for Studying Ur-
     ban Leadership and Policy Outputs: A Brief Cri-
     tique." Journal of Comparative Administration 4
     (February): 429-436.

155 Bachrach, Peter, and Morton Baratz. 1963. "Deci-
     sions and Nondecisions: An Analytical Framework."

American Political Science Review 57 (September): 632-642.

A review of the concepts of power, influence, manipulation and force. The concept of nondecision-making is also introduced. A nondecision is one where the existing power relations between groups prevent certain events from becoming explicit issues where a decision is made.

156 _____, and _____. 1970. Power and Poverty: Theory and Practice. New York: Oxford University Press.

157 Clark, Terry Nichols. 1973. "Citizen Values, Power, and Policy Outputs: A Model of Community Decision-Making." Journal of Comparative Administration 4 (February): 385-427.

158 _____. 1971. "Community Decisions and Budget Expenditures: Toward a Theory of Collective Decision-Making." Unpublished paper presented at the meeting of the American Sociological Association.

159 _____. 1971. "Reflections on the Symposium." In Future Directions in Community Power Research: A Colloquium, edited by Frederick M. Wirt. Berkeley: Institute for Governmental Studies, University of California, Berkeley. 201-224.

160 _____, and William Kornblum. 1967. "Community Values, Decision-Making, and Outputs: Configurations of Innovation and Activeness." International Studies of Values in Politics USA paper no. 84.

161 _____, and James W. Wagner, Jr. 1967. "Community Values, Decision-Making, and Outputs: Configurations of Inactiveness." International Studies of Values in Politics USA paper no. 83.

162 Frey, Frederick W. 1971. "Comment: On Issues and Nonissues in the Study of Power." American Political Science Review 65 (December): 1081-1101.

163 Jamous, Haroun. 1968. "Elements pour une Theorie Sociologique des Décisions Politiques" [Elements for a Sociological Theory of Political Decisions]. Revue Française de Sociologie 9 (Jan.-Mar.): 71-88.

0 164 Jasinska, A.   1967.   "Psychospoleczne Cechy Dziallaczy
         Lokalnych" [Psycho-Sociological Determinants of De-
         cisions].   Studia Socjologiczno Polityczne 23: 45-66.
         Scales were devised to measure and isolate the
         psycho-sociological characteristics of local elites.

O 165 Jennings, M. Kent.   1962.   "Study of Community De-
         cision-Making. "   In Current Trends in Comparative
         Community Studies, edited by Bert Swanson.   Kansas
         City, Mo. : Community Studies, Inc.   18-30.

0 166 Lasswell, Harold.   1963.   "The Decision Process:
         Seven Categories of Functional Analysis. "   In Poli-
         tics and Social Life, edited by Nelson Polsby,
         Robert Dentler, and Paul Smith.   Boston: Houghton
         Mifflin.   93-105.

0 167 Leif, Irving P.   1974.   "A Model of Community De-
         cision-Making and Policy Outputs: New Directions
         for Community Power Theory. "   Unpublished Ph. D.
         dissertation, Temple University.

O 168 Levin, P. H.   1972.   "On Decisions and Decision
         Making. "   Public Administration 50 (Spring): 19-44.

O 169 Long, Norton E.   1966.   "Community Decision-Making. "
         In Community Leadership and Decision-Making, ed. by
         C. R. Adrian.   Iowa City: Institute of Public Af-
         fairs, University of Iowa.   1-10.

0 170 _____.   1962.   "Who Makes Decisions in Metropoli-
         tan Areas ?"   In The Polity, by Norton Long and
         edited by Charles Press.   Chicago: Rand McNally.
         156-164.

321.8
P887p   171 Miller, Delbert C.   1961.   "Democracy and Decision-
              Making in the Community Power Structure. "   In
              Power and Democracy in America, edited by William
              V. D'Antonio and Howard J. Ehrlich.   Notre Dame,
              Ind. : University of Notre Dame Press.   25-71.

O 172 _____.   1957.   "The Predictions of Issue Outcome
         in Community Decision-Making. "   Proceedings of
         The Pacific Sociological Society 25 (June): 137-147.

O 173 Miller, Paul.   1952.   "The Process of Decision-Making
         Within the Context of Community Organization. "

Rural Sociology 17 (June): 153-161.
Decision-making must be looked at through different perspectives in different parts of the country.
In the southeast, community structure and constituted
authority are most important while in the northeast
social psychological components of influence are
most important.

174 Nuttall, Ronald L., Erwin K. Scheuch, and Chad Gordon. 1968. "On the Structure of Influence." In
Community Structure and Decision-Making: Comparative Analyses, edited by Terry N. Clark. San
Francisco: Chandler Pub. Co. 349-380.

175 _____, _____, and _____. 1965. "On the
Structure of Influence." Unpublished paper pre-
sented at the meeting of the Eastern Sociological
Association.

176 Overly, Don H. 1967. "Decision-Making in City
Government: A Proposal." Urban Affairs Quarterly
3 (December): 41-53.

177 Rothenberg, Jerome. 1965. "A Model of Economic
and Political Decision-Making." In The Public
Economy of Urban Communities, edited by Julius
Margolis. Washington, D.C.: Resources for the
Future. 1-38.

178 Shubik, M. 1958. "Studies and Theories of Decision-
Making." Administrative Science Quarterly 3 (December): 283-306.

179 Simon, Herbert. 1959. "Theories of Decision-Making
in Economics and Behavioral-Science." American
Economic Review 49 (June): 253-283.

180 Subramaniam, V. 1963. "Fact and Value in Decision-
Making." Public Administration Review 23 (December): 232-237.
An examination of Herbert Simon's model of decision-making. Subramaniam then suggests his own
four step model which combines facts and values.

181 Wildavsky, Aaron. 1962. "The Analysis of Issue-Con-
texts in the Study of Decision-Making." Journal of
Politics 24 (November): 717-732.

An attempt to show that the analyses of issue-
contexts can be used in developing propositions
about decision-making.

182 Wolfinger, Raymond E.   1971.   " 'Nondecisions' and
the Study of Local Politics. " American Political
Science Review 65 (December):   1063-1080.

183 _____.   1971.   "Rejoinder to Frey's 'Comment'. "
American Political Science Review 65 (December):
1102-1104.

POLITICAL PARTICIPATION

184 Agger, Robert E.   1954.   "The Dynamics of Local
Political Participation: Empirical Research and
Theoretical Inquiry. " Unpublished Ph. D. disserta-
tion, University of Oregon.

185 _____, and Vincent Ostrom.   1956.   "Political Participation in a Small Community. " In Political Behavior: A Reader in Theory and Research, edited
by Heinz Eulau, Samuel J. Eldersveld, and Morris
Janowitz.   Glencoe, Ill. :   The Free Press.   138-
148.

186 Akimoto, Ritsuro.   1970.   "Community Power Structure and Citizen Movement. " Shakaigaku Hyoron 21
(September):   39-49.
Akimoto examined the relationship of participation,
formation, and organization of citizen movements
and their relationship to community power structures.

187 Alford, Robert R.   1968.   "Sources of Local Political
Involvement. " American Political Science Review
62 (December):   1192-1206.
The most important personal characteristics in
local political involvement were social status and
organizational activity.   Less important were civic
duty, political efficacy, political alienation, and local
political environment.   No importance at all was
attached to geographic mobility, length of residence,
and subjective attachment to the community.

188 _____, and Harry M. Scoble.   1968.   "Community

Leadership, Education, and Political Behavior."
American Sociological Review 33 (April): 191-209.
Alford and Scoble found that leadership was more
important than education as a variable in political
involvement. Education was more important in the
formation of political beliefs and ideologies. Community leaders reflected the attitudes of the strata from
which they are drawn.

189 Bosworth, Karl A. 1958. "The Manager Is a Politi-
cian." Public Administration Review 18 (Summer):
216-222.

190 Devereux, Edward C. 1960. "Community Participation and Leadership." Journal of Social Issues 16:
29-45.
A study of the participation of the residents of a
small community and the relationship between participation and leadership.

191 Ditz, Gerhard. 1973. "Citizen Participation in Urban
Politics." Unpublished paper presented at the meeting of the American Sociological Association.

192 Erbe, William W. 1964. "Social Involvement and
Political Activity." American Sociological Review
29 (April): 198-215.
Socio-economic status and organizational involvement are important antecedents to political participation. Erbe argues that the question of alienation
and political involvement is still an unanswered question.

193 Foskett, John M. 1955. "Social Structure and Social
Participation." American Sociological Review 20
(August): 431-438.
Differential social participation was attributed to
occupational roles, the expectations of others, and
the social and technical skills that are associated
with certain social and economic levels.

194 Hall, Nelson E., and Kent P. Schwirlan. 1968. "Occupational Situs, Community Structure, and Local
Political Participation." Sociological Focus 1
(Spring): 17-30.
This study found a high rate of consistency between participation in local politics and occupational
situs.

195   Kornhauser, William. 1959. "Power and Participation
      in the Local Community." Health Education Journal
      6: 28-40.

196   Kuroda, A., and Y. Kuroda. 1968. "Aspects of Com-
      munity Political Participation in Japan." Journal of
      Asian Studies 27 (February): 229-251.

197   Kuroda, Yasumasa. 1967. "Measurement Correlates
      and Significance of Political Participation in a Japan-
      ese Community." Western Political Quarterly 20
      (September): 660-668.
          Kuroda found that citizen participation in a Japan-
      ese local community was similar to the citizen par-
      ticipation of Americans. Sex, education, and other
      sociological and psychological variables and their re-
      lationship to political participation was similar to the
      findings of American studies.

198   Lane, Robert E. 1966. "The Decline of Politics and
      Ideology in a Knowledgeable Society." American
      Sociological Review 31 (October): 649-662.
          Lane argues that the scope of politics is shrinking
      while the scope of knowledge is growing. This has
      created different perspectives among policy-makers.
      Because of the growth of knowledge, ideology is de-
      clining as a necessary ingredient in change.

199   Lindenfeld, Frank. 1961. "An Analysis of Political
      Involvement." Unpublished Ph.D. dissertation,
      Columbia University.

200   _____. 1964. "Economic Interest and Political In-
      volvement." Public Opinion Quarterly 28 (Spring):
      104-111.
          Individual economic interest is not found to be a
      factor contributing to political involvement. Eco-
      nomic self-interest is furthered through the leader-
      ship of the social groups to which various individuals
      belong.

201   Nimmo, Dan, and Clifton McCleskey. 1971. "Voter
      Qualification and Participation in National, State and
      Municipal Elections: The Case of Houston, Texas."
      In Community Politics: A Behavioral Approach,
      edited by Charles M. Bonjean, Terry N. Clark, and
      Robert L. Lineberry. New York: The Free Press.
      106-114.

202 Powell, S. 1969. "Political Participation in the Bar-
     riadas: A Case Study." Comparative Political
     Studies 2 (July): 195-215.

203 Rorkan, Stein. 1962. "Approaches to the Study of
     Political Participation: Introduction." Acta Sociol-
     ogica 6: 1-8.

204 Rose, Arnold M., and Caroline Rose. 1951. "Com-
     munication and Participation in a Small City as
     Viewed by Its Leaders." International Journal of
     Opinion and Attitude Research 5 (Fall): 367-390.

205 Sigal, Silvia. 1967. "Participación y Sociedad Na-
     cional: El Caso de las Communidades Rurales
     Latinoamericanas" [Participation and National So-
     ciety: The Case of Latin American Rural Commu-
     nities]. Revista Latinoamericana de Sociologia 3
     (July): 232-289.

206 Smith, Lincoln. 1955. "Town Meeting Government."
     Social Science 30 (June): 174-185.

207 Sower, Christopher, John Holland, Kenneth Tiedtke, and
     Walter Freeman. 1957. Community Involvement.
     Glencoe, Ill.: The Free Press.

208 _____, and Walter Freeman. 1958. "Community
     Involvement in Community Development Programs."
     Rural Sociology 23 (March): 25-33.
         A study of community involvement in order to
     achieve community and national goals. Sower and
     Freeman found that the involvement process went
     through three stages: recognition of problem situa-
     tions, the value forming process, and the stage of
     participation.

209 Swanson, Bert E. 1956. "The Role of the Political
     Party and Its Participants in the Community: An
     Exploratory Field Study." Unpublished M.A. Thesis,
     University of Oregon.

210 Wilson, Everett K. 1954. "Determinants of Participa-
     tion in Policy Formation in a College Community."
     Human Relations 7 (August): 287-312.

211 Zikmund, Joseph, and Robert Smith. 1969. "Political

Participation in an Upper-Middle Class Suburb."
Urban Affairs Quarterly 4 (June): 443-458.

LOCAL GOVERNMENT STRUCTURE

212 Agger, Robert, and Daniel Goldrich. 1958. "Community Power Structures and Partisanship." American
Sociological Review 23 (August): 383-392.
A study of partisan effects on the power structure
of two communities which were legally nonpartisan.
The extent of partisanship was determined by the affiliations of the leaders of the power structure and
the extent to which members of the other partisan
groups could gain entry to it.

213 _____, Bert Swanson, Daniel Goldrich, and Marshall
N. Goldstein. 1962. "Political Influence Structures:
Some Theoretical and Empirical Considerations." In
Current Trends in Community Studies, edited by
Bert Swanson, Kansas City, Mo.: Community
Studies, Inc. 81-88.

214 Aiken, Michael. 1970. ("The Distribution of Community
Power:) Structural and Social Consequences." In
The Structure of Community Power, edited by
Michael Aiken and Paul Mott. New York: Random
House. 487-525.

215 Akpan, E. E. 1965. "The Development of Local Government in Eastern Nigeria." Journal of Local Administration Overseas 4 (April): 118-127.

216 Alford, Robert R., and Leo Schnore. 1963. "Forms
of Government and Socioeconomic Characteristics of
Suburbs." Administrative Science Quarterly 8 (June):
1-17.

217 Banfield, Edward C. 1957. "The Politics of Metropolitan Area Organization." Midwest Journal of Political Science 1 (May): 77-91.

218 Banwell, H. 1963. "The Machinery of Local Government: The Creaks." Public Administration 41 (Winter): 335-344.
Banwell does not believe that local government

has adjusted to modern needs.   He calls for more
cooperation between central and local governments.

219   Bard, A. A. de.   1960.   "Council-Manager Government in Halifax."   Canadian Public Administration
3 (March):   76-81.

220   Bhattacharya, M.   1968.   "Structure of Urban Local
Government in India."   Journal of Local Administration Overseas 7 (April):   351-357.
Urban government is still in the formative stages
in India.   This is due in large measure to the apathy
of the urban communities themselves as well as the
failure of the states to improve them.   Bhattacharya
argues that the states should bear the responsibility
for improving local government.

221   Blackwell, Gordon W.   1954.   "A Theoretical Framework for Sociological Research in Community Organization."   Social Forces 33 (October):   57-64.

222   Bockman, Sheldon E.   1968.   "Power and Decision-
Making Within and Between Institutional Sectors:
The Differential Impact by Issues on Institutional
Sectors."   Unpublished Ph. D. dissertation, Indiana
University.
It is argued that the community's decision-making
system is made up of fundamental units called institutional sectors.   These institutional sectors were
conceptualized as a steady clustering of groups
around a specific institutional value activity.   Each
sector generates a specific, but varying amount of
power in the decision-making process.

223   Boskoff, Alvin.   1968.   Urban Power Structures and
the Management of Innovation: A Typology and Related Theoretical Deductions."   Unpublished paper
presented at the meeting of the American Sociological Association.

224   Brown, R. T.   1960.   "Local Government in the African
Areas in Kenya."   Journal of African Administration
12 (July):   147-149.

225   Cahill, R. S. , and H. J. Friedman.   1964.   "Criteria
for a Proposed Theory of Local Government."
Philippine Journal of Public Administration 8
(October):   288-302.

226 Campbell, M. J. , T. G. Brierly, and L. F. Blitz.
1965. The Structure of Local Government in West
Africa. The Hague: Martinus Nijhoff.

227 Cappelletti, L. 1963. "Local Government in Italy."
Public Administration 41 (Autumn): 247-264.

228 Cardenas, Leonard, Jr. 1965. "Contemporary Problems of Local Government in Mexico." Western
Political Quarterly 18 (December): 858-865.

229 Cattell, D. T. 1964. "Local Government and the
Sovnarkhoz in the U. S. S. R. , 1957-1962." Soviet
Studies 15 (April): 430-442.

230 Churchward, L. G. 1960. "Lokalverwaltung und Rate
in der Sovjetunion seit dem XX. Parteikongress"
[Local Government and Councils in the Soviet Union
Since the XXth Congress of the Communist Party].
Osteuropa 10 (janv.): 5-14.

231 Clark, Terry N. 1967. Community or Communities--
A Dilemma for Studies of Community Power." Kansas Journal of Sociology 3 (Winter): 1-11.

232 _____. 1970. "On Decentralization." Polity 2
(Summer): 508-514.

233 Clarke, J. J. 1969. Outlines of Local Government
of the United Kingdom. London: Pittman.

234 Committee for Economic Development. 1966. Modern-
izing Local Government. New York: Committee
for Economic Development.

235 _____. 1971. Reshaping Government in Metropolitan Areas. New York: Committee for Economic
Development.

236 Costello, Timothy W. 1971. "Change in Municipal
Government: A View From the Inside." The
Journal of Applied Behavioral Science 7 (March/
April): 131-145.

237 Dahl, Robert. 1957. "Some Notes and Models for
Political Systems." Unpublished paper presented
at the SSRC Seminar on Urban Leadership.

238 Djordjevic, Jovan, and N. Pasic. 1961. "Le Système
de Self-Government Communal in Yougoslavie" [The
System of Local Self-Government in Yugoslavia].
Revue Internationale des Sciences Sociales 13: 411-
430.

239 Donald, C. L. 1960. "Brazilian Local Self-Government: Myth or Reality?" Western Political Quarterly 13 (December): 1043-1055.

240 Dudley, Charles J., Harold L. Nix, and Frederick L.
Bates. 1966. "Community Power Structure: A
Structural Approach." Unpublished paper presented
at the meeting of the Southern Sociological Society.

241 Fesler, James. 1965. "Approaches to the Understanding of Decentralization." Journal of Politics 27
(August): 536-566.

242 Field, Arthur J. 1967. "The Community Is the
Power Structure." Unpublished paper presented
at the meeting of the American Sociological Association.

243 _____. 1970. Urban Power Structures. Cambridge,
Mass.: Schenkman Publishing Company.

244 Friesema, H. Paul. 1966. "The Metropolis and the
Maze of Local Government." Urban Affairs Quarterly 2 (December): 68-90.
Friesema argues that there has not been sufficient interpretations of metropolitan political structures.

245 Gosciniak, K. 1960. "Reorganizacja Systemu Tereno-
wych Orgonow Wladzy Panstwowej w Bulgarskiej"
[The Reorganization of the System of Local Government Authorities in Bulgaria]. Pavstivo i Prawo
15 (Nov.): 799-809.

246 Grant, Daniel R. 1954. "Federal Municipal Relationships and Metropolitan Integration." Public Administration Review 14 (Autumn): 259-267.

247 _____. 1968. "The Metropolitan Government Approach: Should, Can, and Will It Prevail?" Urban
Affairs Quarterly 3 (March): 103-110.

248 Gupta, S. P. , and J. P. Hutton. 1969. "Local Gov-
     ernment Efficiency--What Is It?" Local Government
     Finance 73 (July): 278-281.

249 Harz, J. W. 1965. "Z Badan nad Rola Czynnika
     Spolecznego w Systemie Wladzy Terenowej" [The
     Role of Representative Bodies in the System of
     Local Government]. Studia Socjologiczno Polityczne
     19: 7-38.

250 Healey, A. M. 1961. "Native Local Government in
     New Guinea: Its Functions and Problems." Journal
     of African Administration 13 (July): 165-174.

251 Hofmann, W. 1968. "Demokratie und Effektivitat in
     der englischen Kommunalverwaltung" [Democracy and
     Efficiency in English Local Government]. Archiv
     für Kommunalwissenschaften 7: 100-109.

252 Holck, P. 1962. "Traek fra en Lokal Forvaltning"
     [Trends of Local Administration]. Nordisk Admin-
     istrativt Tidsskrift 43: 23-29.

253 Hughes, P. 1963. "The Introduction of Local Govern-
     ment to Basutoland." Journal of Local Adminis-
     tration Overseas 2 (July): 154-159.

254 Hunter, Floyd. 1958. "Studying Associations and Or-
     ganizational Structure." In Approaches to the Study
     of Politics, edited by Roland Young. Evanston, Ill.:
     Northwestern University Press. 343-363.

255 Institute of Public Administration, University of the
     Philippines. 1959. "The System of Local Govern-
     ment in the Philippines." Philippine Journal of
     Public Administration 3 (January): 7-10.

256 International Union of Local Authorities. 1963. Local
     Government in the XXth Century. The Hague: Mar-
     tinus Nijhoff.

257 Izmirlian, H. , Jr. 1968. "The Implications of Politi-
     cal Structure for Economic Behavior--A Study in the
     Communication of Ideas." Asian Survey 8 (Novem-
     ber): 911-920.

258 Jackson, William Eric. 1966. The Structure of Local

Government in England and Wales. London: Long-
mans Green.

259 Jacob, Phillip E., and James V. Toscano, editors.
     1964. The Integration of Political Communities.
     Philadelphia: Lippincott.

260 Jenkins, W. J. 1967. Local Government in Britain.
     Oxford: Pergamon Press.

261 Jerovsek, Janez. 1966. "Kontrola u Lokalnoj Zajed-
     nici" [Control in the Local Community]. Sociologija
     Sela 4 (Jan.-Jun.): 143-150.
     A study of the role of the distribution of power
     in local communities. The intensity of social con-
     trol depends on the size of the local community.

262 Johnson, Rogers P. 1968. "Community, Democracy,
     and Power: A Study of Conflicting Themes in the
     Sociological Conception of Community." Unpublished
     Ph.D. dissertation, Brandeis University.

263 Joiner, Charles A. 1964. Organizational Analysis:
     Political, Sociological, and Administrative Processes
     of Local Government. East Lansing: Institute for
     Community Development and Services, Michigan
     State University.

264 Jonassen, Christen T. 1959. "Community Typology."
     In Community Structure and Analysis, edited by
     Marvin Sussman. New York: Thomas Y. Crowell.
     15-36.

265 Kaufman, Harold F., and Kenneth P. Wilkinson. 1967.
     Community Structure and Leadership: An Interactive
     Perspective in the Study of Community. State Col-
     lege, Mississippi: Mississippi State University So-
     cial Science Research Center Bulletin 13 (June).

266 Keith-Lucas, Bryan. 1961. "Metropolitan Local Gov-
     ernment in Canada." Public Administration 39
     (Autumn): 251-262.

267 Kessel, John H. 1962. "Government Structure and
     Political Environment: A Statistical Note About
     American Cities." American Political Science Re-
     view 56 (September): 615-620.

268 Khan, I. H.   1969. "Local Government in Rural India."
     Australian Journal of Political History 15 (Decem-
     ber): 11-25.

269 Kilson, M.   1964. "Grass-Roots Politics in Africa:
     Local Government in Sierra Leone."   Political
     Studies 12 (February): 47-66.

270 Kojima, R.   1961. "Local Government in Japan."
     EROPA Review 1 (October): 77-84.

271 Leemans, A. F.   1970.   Changing Patterns of Local
     Government.   The Hague: International Union of
     Local Authorities.

272 Lofts, D.   1959.   "The Future Pattern of Local Gov-
     ernment in England and Wales." Public Adminis-
     tration 37 (Autumn): 275-292.

273 Mantel, Howard N.   1970. "Reorganization of New
     York City Government."   Public Administration
     48 (Summer): 191-212.   A proposal for the reor-
     ganization of the New York City government.

274 Miller, Kenneth Edward.   1965.   "The Structural Cor-
     relates of Community Power Systems." Unpublished
     Ph. D. dissertation, Duke University.

275 Morlan, Robert L.   1964.   "Cabinet Government at the
     Municipal Level: The Dutch Experience."   Western
     Political Quarterly 17 (June): 317-324.

276 Mulford, Charles L.   1962.   "Some Relationships Be-
     tween Formal Organizations, Community Problems,
     and Leadership." Unpublished Ph. D. dissertation,
     Iowa State University of Science and Technology.

277 Nolting, Orin F.   1958.   "The Council-Manager Plan
     in Europe." Public Management 40 (May): 110-114.

278 Ostrom, Elinor.   1972.   "Metropolitan Reform: Prop-
     ositions Derived From Two Traditions."   Social
     Science Quarterly 53 (December): 474-493.

279 _____.   1971.   "Metropolitan Reform: Propositions
     Derived From Two Traditions." Unpublished paper
     presented at the meeting of the Society for the Study
     of Social Problems.

280 Ostrom, Vincent, Charles Tiebout, and Robert Warren.
     1961. "The Organization of Government in Metro-
     politan Areas: A Theoretical Inquiry." American
     Political Science Review 55 (December): 831-842.
          An inquiry into the feasibility of a polycentric
     political system for the purpose of governing metro-
     politan areas.

281 Ramayan, Prasad. 1963. Local Self-Government in
     Vindhya Pradesh. Bombay: All-India Institute of
     Local Self-Government.

282 Rehfuss, John A. 1968. "Metropolitan Government:
     Four Views." Urban Affairs Quarterly 3 (June):
     91-111.

283 Robson, William A. 1966. Local Government in Cri-
     sis. London: George Allen & Unwin.

284 Rodrigues, M. R. 1962. "Local Government in Ja-
     maica." Journal of Local Administration Overseas
     1 (April): 102-111.

285 Rogers, David. 1964. "Monolithic and Pluralistic
     Community Power Structures." In Social Organiza-
     tion and Behavior, edited by R. L. Simpson and
     I. H. Simpson. New York: John Wiley. 400-405.

286 Rossi, Peter. 1961. "The Organizational Structure of
     an American Community." In Complex Organiza-
     tions: A Sociological Reader, edited by Amitai
     Etzioni. New York: Holt, Rinehart & Winston.
     301-312.

287 _____. 1960. "Power and Community Structure."
     Midwest Journal of Political Science 4 (November):
     390-401.
          The structural characteristics of communities
     were examined specifically in relation to their power
     structures. Rossi concludes that the pattern of
     power in a community is a function of its political
     life and the relationship between governmental insti-
     tutions and the electorate.

288 _____. 1959. "A Theory of Community Structures."
     Unpublished paper presented at the meeting of the
     American Sociological Society.

289 _____. 1960. "Theory, Research, and Practice in
Community Organization." In Social Science and
Community Action, edited by Charles R. Adrian.
East Lansing: Michigan State University Press.
9-24.

290 _____, and Phillips Cutright. 1961. "The Political
Organization of an Industrial Community." In Com-
munity Political Systems, edited by Morris Janowitz.
Glencoe, Ill.: The Free Press. 81-116.

291 Schildkrout, E. 1970. "Strangers and Local Government in Kumasi." Journal of Modern African Studies
8 (July): 251-269.

292 Scoble, Harry M. 1971. "Where the Pluralists Went
Wrong." In Future Directions in Community Power
Research: A Colloquium, edited by Frederick M.
Wirt. Berkeley: Institute for Governmental Studies,
University of California, Berkeley. 105-124.

293 Scott, Thomas M. 1968. "Metropolitan Governmental
Reorganization Proposals." Western Political Quarterly 2 (June): 252-261.
     Normal metropolitan areas will not respond to
government reorganization with radical changes.
Radical reorganization takes place only in areas
with unusual social, political, and economic characteristics.

294 Sharp, E. 1962. "The Future of Local Government."
Public Administration 40 (Winter): 375-386.

295 Singh, P. 1969. "The Development of Local Government in the Commonwealth Caribbean." Studies in
Comparative Local Government (Summer): 28-40.

296 _____. 1970. "Problems of Institutional Transplan-
tation: The Case of the Commonwealth Caribbean
Local Government System." Caribbean Studies 10
(April): 22-23.

297 Soysal, M. 1967. Local Government in Turkey.
Ankara: Institute of Public Administration for Turkey and the Middle East.

298 Steiner, Kurt. 1965. Local Government in Japan.

Stanford, Cal.: Stanford University Press.

299 Stephens, G. Ross. 1971. "The Power Grid of the
     Metropolis." In Future Directions in Community
     Power Research: A Colloquium, edited by Freder-
     ick M. Wirt. Berkeley: Institute for Governmental
     Studies, University of California, Berkeley. 125-145.

300 Stojanovic, A. 1961. "Lokalna Uprava u Engleskoi"
     [Local Self-Government in Great Britain]. Anali
     Pravnog Fakulteta u Beogradu 9 (Apr.-Sept.): 191-
     207.

301 Stone, Gregory, and William H. Form. 1953. "In-
     stabilities in Status: The Problem of Hierarchy in
     the Community Study of Status Arrangements."
     American Sociological Review 8 (April): 149-162.

302 Suski, Julian G. 1965. "The Structure of Municipal
     Government in Canada and in Europe." Canadian
     Public Administration 8 (September): 307-324.

303 Sussman, Marvin B., editor. 1959. Community Struc-
     ture and Analysis. New York: Thomas Y. Crowell.

304 Swaffield, J. C. 1970. "Local Government in the Na-
     tional Setting." Public Administration 48 (Autumn):
     307-315.

305 Wallis, C. A. G. 1961. "Local Administration in the
     Sudan." Journal of African Administration 13 (July):
     158-164.

306 _____. 1963. "Urgent Local Government Problems
     in Africa." Journal of Local Administration Over-
     seas 2 (April): 61-74.

307 Walton, John. 1968. "Differential Patterns of Commu-
     nity Power Structure: An Explanation Based on In-
     terdependence." Sociological Quarterly 9 (Winter):
     3-18.
         An explanation of Warren's vertical axis of com-
     munity organization based on a secondary analysis of
     community power studies. Walton concluded that the
     introduction of extra-community influences produces
     a "fragmentation of local normative order."

308   _____. 1968. "Normative Order and Change in Or-
         ganization of Community Power: A Comment."
         Southwestern Social Science Quarterly 48 (April):
         636-638.

309   _____. 1967. "The Vertical Axis of Community
         Organization and the Structure of Power." South-
         western Social Science Quarterly 48 (December):
         353-368.
             A theory of local community and extra-community
         influence was introduced. It was posited that the
         greater the influence of extra-community culture and
         groups, the more fragmented the local political sys-
         tem will become. The greater the vertical axis, the
         greater the pluralism of the political system.

310   Warren, Roland L. 1967. "Interaction of Community
         Decision Organizations: Some Basic Concepts and
         Needed Research." Social Service Review 4 (Sep-
         tember): 261-270.
             Studying community decision organizations can be
         done on two levels; the interactions of the organi-
         zation within itself and the interaction of the organi-
         zation with other organizations. Warren's calls for
         more research on interorganizational behavior.

311   _____. 1967. "A Note on Walton's Analysis of
         Power Structure and Vertical Ties." Southwestern
         Social Science Quarterly 48 (December): 369-372.
             Warren generally is in agreement with Walton's
         thesis of vertical ties and community power. War-
         ren's main point is the discussion of community
         autonomy which produces monolithic structures as
         opposed to vertical ties which produce pluralist and
         fragmented structures.

312   Wettenhall, R. L. 1962. "Tasmanian Local Govern-
         ment at the Crossroads." Public Administration 21
         (December): 378-387.

313   Whalen, H. 1960. "Democracy and Local Government."
         Canadian Public Administration 3 (March): 1-13.

314   _____. 1960. "Ideology, Democracy and the Foun-
         dations of Local Self-Government." Canadian Jour-
         nal of Economics and Political Science 26 (August):
         377-395.

315 Wiatr, Jerzy J. 1967. "Industrializacja Socjalistyczna
     --System Polityczny--Zagadnievia Wladzy Lokalnej"
     [Socialist Industrialization. The Political System--
     The Local System]. Studia Socjologiczno Polityczne
     23: 13-27.
          The formal legal relationships between the central
     and local power structures were examined. The in-
     fluence of the socialist industrialization on power
     structures was also examined.

316 Wolfinger, Raymond E. , and John Osgood Field. 1968.
     "Political Ethos and the Structure of City Govern-
     ment." In Community Structure and Decision-Mak-
     ing: Comparative Analyses, edited by Terry N.
     Clark. San Francisco: Chandler Pub. Co. 159-
     196.

317 Wraith, Ronald E. 1964. Local Government in West
     Africa. New York: Praeger.

318 Yao, C. C. 1961. "Local Self-Government in South-
     East Asia. " EROPA Review 1 (June): 51-103.

319 Young, Ruth, and Olaf Larson. 1965. "A New Ap-
     proach to Community Structure. " American Socio-
     logical Review 30 (December): 926-934.
          The findings of this study demonstrate that sub-
     communities can be studied in the context of overall
     community structure. It becomes possible through
     this method to study the role of sub-communities
     and community leadership.

320 Zimmerman, Joseph F. 1970. "Metropolitan Reform
     in the U. S. A. : An Overview. " Public Administra-
     tion Review 30 (September/October): 531-543.
          The failure of factionalized local government to
     reorganize was attributed to political inertia and the
     failure of federal and state governments to provide
     the rationale of the government of metropolitan areas.

2

METHODOLOGY OF COMMUNITY POWER STUDIES

GENERAL METHODOLOGICAL STUDIES

321 Agger, Robert E. 1966. "Panel Studies of Comparative Political Decision Making: Dynamics of Urban Renewal." In The Electoral Process, edited by M. Kent Jennings and L. Harmon Ziegler. Englewood Cliffs, N. J.: Prentice-Hall. 265-289.

322 Arensberg, Conrad C. 1954. "The Community Study Method." American Journal of Sociology 60 (September): 109-124.
    Arensberg re-examined the community study method and found it to be a useful research tool.

323 Bassett, Raymond E. 1948. "Sampling Problems in Influence Studies." Sociometry 12 (November): 320-328.

324 Bauman, Z. 1962. "Struktura Wladzy Spolecznosci Lokalnej" [Patterns of Power in a Local Community]. Studia Socjologiczno Polityczne 12: 7-30.
    Bauman proposed a five-stage procedure for use in community power research in Poland. This procedure included identifying the elite through documents, through the study of the formal political structure, through the identification of influence elites, through a study of cultural community decisions, and finally through the development of a schema of the local power structure based on data collected through the first four procedures.

325 Beck, C., and J. M. Mallory. 1966. "Elite Politicas: Um Metodo de Analise" [Political Elites: A Method of Analysis]. Revista de Direito Publico e Ciencia Politica 9 (Avr. -Juin): 70-109.

40

326 Blackwell, Gordon W. 1958. "Community Analysis."
In Approaches to the Study of Politics, edited by
Roland Young. Evanston, Ill.: Northwestern Uni-
versity Press. 305-317.

327 Blankenship, L. Vaughn. 1964. "Community Power
and Decision-Making: A Comparative Evaluation of
Measurement Techniques." Social Forces 43 (December): 207-216.
A comparison of the reputational technique and
the decision-making technique for measuring power.
The results showed that basically the same leadership group emerged using the two techniques across
two communities.

328 Boek, Walter. 1965. "Field Techniques in Delineating
the Structure of Community Leadership." Human
Organization 24 (Winter): 358-364.
Boek proposed using an anthropological method of
mapping interactions during real community events
to delineate the power structure of communities.

329 Booth, David A., and Charles R. Adrian. 1961. "Sim-
plifying the Discovery of Elites." American Behavioral Scientist 5 (October): 14-16.
A test of the Miller-Form technique for identifying community leaders was undertaken. The authors
conclude that the Miller-Form technique is reliable.

330 Carstenson, Blue Alan. 1956. "A Method for Studying
How People Perceive Power Structure in Their Communities as Tested in Five Michigan Communities."
Unpublished Ph.D. dissertation, University of Michigan.

331 Clark, Terry N. 1972. "Urban Typologies and Political Outputs." In Handbook of City Classification,
edited by B. J. L. Berry. New York: John Wiley
& Sons. 152-178.

332 _____. 1970. "Urban Typologies and Political Out-
puts: Causal Models Using Discrete Variables and
Orthogonal Factors, Or, Precise Distortion Versus
Model Muddling." Social Science Information 9
(December): 7-33.

333 D'Antonio, William V., Howard Ehrlich, and Eugene

Erickson.   1962.   "Further Notes on the Study of
Community Power."   American Sociological Review
27 (December):   848-853.
A rebuttal to the arguments of Polsby and Wolfinger.   Also, a call for a more concentrated effort
to critique the decision-making technique for studying community power structures.

334   Dick, Harry R.   1960.   "A Method for Ranking Community Influentials."   American Sociological Review 25
(June):   395-399.
Dick argues that the problems incurred in the
use of the reputational technique for measuring
power are the same problems that arise in attitude
scaling.   He suggests that these problems can be
solved effectively with the use of Guttman type scaling and image analysis.

335   Fox, Douglas M.   1971.   "A Comparison of Different
Methods Used to Study Community Power."   Rural
Sociology 36 (March):   56-58.
A comparison of the findings of the positional,
decisional, and reputational techniques for identifying
power structures when used simultaneously in power
studies.   Fox concludes that different methods do
not necessarily reveal the same community power
structure when used jointly in the same community.

336   _____.   1969.   "The Identification of Community
Leaders by the Reputational and Decisional Methods:
Three Case Studies and an Empirical Analysis of
the Literature."   Sociology and Social Research 54
(October):   94-103.
While the reputational and decisional techniques
do not necessarily yield the same leadership group,
it does not mean that they uncover different kinds of
power structures.

337   _____.   1971.   "Method Within Methods: The Case
of Community Power Studies."   Western Political
Quarterly 24 (March):   5-11.
Fox contends that the reputational and decision-
making approaches used in uncovering community
power structures is actually four approaches.   The
variants of these approaches may yield results so
different that comparisons may not be possible.

338   French, Robert Mills. 1969. "Effectiveness of Vari-
       ous Techniques in the Study of Community Power."
       Journal of Politics 31 (August): 818-820.
            French found that the reputational technique com-
       bined with the positional technique was very effec-
       tive in locating community leaders. The decision-
       making technique did not uncover any of the signifi-
       cant leaders not revealed by the use of the positional-
       reputational technique.

339   Gittell, Marilyn. 1966. "A Typology of Power for
       Measuring Social Change." The American Behav-
       ioral Scientist 9 (April): 23-28.

340   Golembiewski, Robert T. 1969. "The Wages of
       Methodological Inelegance Is Circularity, II: Elitists
       and Pluralists." In A Methodological Primer for
       Social Scientists, edited by Robert T. Golembiewski
       et al. Chicago: Rand McNally. 149-190.

341   Harkness, Shirley J. 1972. "Field Methodology for
       the Study of Third World Urban Elites: A Colombian
       Example." The Cornell Journal of Social Relations
       7 (Spring): 36-51.

342   Kadushin, Charles. 1968. "Power, Influence, and So-
       cial Circles: A New Methodology for Studying Elites."
       Unpublished paper presented at the meeting of the
       American Political Science Association.

343   _____. 1968. "Power, Influence, and Social Cir-
       cles: A New Methodology for Studying Opinion-
       Makers." American Sociological Review 33 (Octo-
       ber): 685-699.
            Kadushin argues that present definitions of power
       and influence are inadequate. He proposes the use
       of social circles in measuring power output. Snow-
       ball sampling techniques and sociometric chains are
       used to expose these chains of social circles.

344   Kaufman, Herbert, and Victor Jones. 1954. "The
       Mystery of Power." Public Administration Review
       14 (Summer): 205-212.
            This paper is a critique of Hunter's Community
       Power Structure. They criticize Hunter in a variety
       of ways including his selection of a "panel" to choose
       leaders to his presuppositions that there was a

power structure in Atlanta.

345 Kimball, Solon T. , and Marion Pearsall.   1955.
"Event Analysis as an Approach to Community
Study. "   Social Forces 34 (October):   161-168.
Kimball and Pearsall argue for the use of obser-
vations of interactional patterns to determine the
community structure.

346 Laumann, Edward O. , and Franz Urban Pappi.   1973.
"New Directions in the Study of Elites. "   American
Sociological Review 38 (April):   212-230.
A methodological approach was developed based
on graph theory, smallest space analysis, and parts
of the structural analysis of Talcott Parsons.   A
theoretical and empirical scheme was proposed for
community issue identification and tracing issue impact.

347 _____, and _____.   1972.   "New Directions in
the Study of Elites. "   Unpublished paper presented
at the meeting of the American Sociological Association.

348 Mann, Lawrence D.   1964.   "Studies in Community
Decision-Making. "   Journal of the American Institute of Planners 30 (February):   58-65.

349 Mulford, Charles L.   1965.   "Comment on the Identification of Leaders. "   Social Forces 44 (December):
251.
Mulford argues that the concept of 'concealed
leader' (Miller-Dirksen) is better suited for use in
urban communities than in rural communities.

350 Narojek, W.   1962.   "Zalozenia Studium nad Ludzmi
Wladzy Miasteczka" [Guiding Principles for a Study
of Power Groups in a Small Town].   Studia Socjologiczno Polityczne 12:   31-40.
Based on a community power study of Plock,
Narojek argues that power groups should be studied
through the formal power structure, the actual power
structure, a combination of the formal and actual
power structures, and the opinions of the population
concerning their power structure.

351 Phillett, Serena.   1963.   "An Analysis of Community

Influence: Some Conceptual and Methodological Considerations." Unpublished M.A. thesis, University of Alberta, Canada.

352 Polsby, Nelson W. 1962. "Community Power: Some Reflections on the Recent Literature." American Sociological Review 27 (December): 838-841.
     A critique of D'Antonio and Erickson's paper defending the use of the reputational technique.

353 Porter, John. 1955. "Elite Groups: A Scheme for the Study of Power in Canada." Canadian Journal of Economics and Political Science 21 (November): 498-512.

354 Powers, Ronald C. 1965. Identifying the Community Power Structure. Ames: North Central Regional Extension Publication No. 19, NCRS Leadership Series No. 2, Cooperative Extension Service, Iowa State University of Science and Technology.

355 Preston, James D. 1969. "Identification of Community Leaders." Sociology and Social Research 53 (January): 204-216.
     The reputational, participational, and positional techniques for uncovering community power structures were compared. All three approaches identified basically the same set of leaders. Preston suggests that in small and middle-sized cities all three approaches would yield the same results.

356 Riker, W. H. 1959. "A Test of the Adequacy of the Power Index." Behavioral Science 4 (April): 120-131.

357 Rossi, Peter. 1960. "Theory and Method in the Study of Power in the Local Community." Unpublished paper presented at the meeting of the American Sociological Association.

358 _____, and Robert L. Crain. 1968. "The NORC Permanent Community Sample." Public Opinion Quarterly 32 (Summer): 261-272.
     The NORC Permanent Community Sample is a facility set up to collect data for comparative community research. The data archives consist of a probability sample of 200 United States cities with populations over 50,000.

359 Sollie, Carlton R. 1961. "Community Leadership: A
      Critical Survey of the Literature and Formulation of
      Hypotheses." Unpublished master's thesis, Missis-
      sippi State University.

360 Tannenbaum, Arnold. 1962. "An Event Approach to
      Social Power and to the Problem of Comparability."
      Behavioral Science 7 (July): 315-331.

361 Vannan, Donald Antrim. 1962. "Methods of Identifying
      Community Power Structures Utilized by Chief School
      Administrators in Selected School Districts of Penn-
      sylvania." Unpublished Ph. D. dissertation, Penn-
      sylvania State University.

362 Wagner, Stanley, Wayne Viney, Judith McClung, and
      Andrea Larson. 1966. "An Empirical Method for
      the Examination of Power in Oklahoma City." Pro-
      ceedings of the Oklahoma Academy of Science 46:
      166-170.

363 White, James E. 1950. "Theory and Method for Re-
      search in Community Leadership." American Socio-
      logical Review 5 (February): 50-60.
         A New York rural community was used to deter-
      mine correlations between formal and informal leader-
      ship groups and the ability of community workers to
      select them.

364 Wilkinson, Kenneth P. 1965. "A Behavioral Measure
      of Community Leadership." Unpublished Ph. D. dis-
      sertation, Mississippi State University.
         A measure of community leadership was developed
      based on a community role influence score and a
      scope of community influence score. There was a
      high correlation between the behavioral measure and
      the reputational measure.

365 Williams, James Morgan. 1973. "The Ecological Ap-
      proach in Measuring Community Power Concentration:
      An Analysis of Hawley's MPO Ratio." American
      Sociological Review 38 (April): 230-242.

366 _____. 1971. "Structural Correlates of Community
      Power Concentration: An Evaluation of Hawley's
      MPO Ratio." Unpublished Ph. D. dissertation, Uni-
      versity of Texas.

REPUTATIONAL TECHNIQUE

367   Abu-Laban, Baha.   1965.   "The Reputational Approach
       in the Study of Community Power: A Critical Evalu-
       ation. "   Pacific Sociological Review 8 (Spring):   35-
       42.
            Abu-Laban found that critics of the reputational
       technique have failed to realize the objectives of its
       use.   Also, they have judged the reputational tech-
       nique by the decision-making technique without inde-
       pendently validating the decision-making technique.
       Finally, the studies of the reputational technique
       validating its reliability did not arrive fast enough
       to counter criticisms of it.

368   D'Antonio, William V. , and Eugene Erickson.   1962.
       "The Reputational Technique as a Measure of Com-
       munity Power: An Evaluation Based on Comparative
       and Longitudinal Studies. "   American Sociological
       Review 27 (March):   362-376.
            The reputational technique was tested to counter
       the criticisms of theorists such as Dahl, Polsby,
       and Wolfinger.   D'Antonio and Erickson found that
       the reputational technique does measure general com-
       munity influence, is reliable, and does provide the
       researcher with a general picture of the power struc-
       ture of a community.

369   Ehrlich, Howard J.   1961.   "The Reputational Approach
       to the Study of Community Power. "   American
       Sociological Review 26 (December):   926-927.
            Ehrlich answers Wolfinger's criticisms of the
       reputational technique for measuring power.   He
       concluded that Wolfinger's criticisms were not suf-
       ficient to warrant dismissal of the reputational tech-
       nique from use by researchers.

370   _____.   1967.   "The Social Psychology of Reputa-
       tions for Community Leadership. "   Sociological
       Quarterly 8 (Summer):   514-530.
            There was a strong monotonic relationship between
       leadership nominations and socio-economic status
       and community participation of the respondents.

371   Erickson, Eugene C.   1962.   "The Reputational Tech-
       nique in a Cross-Community Perspective: Selected

Problems of Theory and Measurement." Unpublished
Ph. D. dissertation, Michigan State University.

372 Gamson, William. 1966. "Reputation and Resources
in Community Politics." American Journal of
Sociology 72 (September): 121-131.
   Reputation is seen as a resource rather than an
indication of power. In other words, reputation
represents a source of potential power rather than
influence in use.

373 Laskin, Richard, and Serena Phillett. 1964. "Formal
Versus Reputational Leadership Identification: A
Re-evaluation." Unpublished paper presented at the
meeting of the Pacific Sociological Association.

374 _____, and _____. 1965. "An Integrative Analysis of Voluntary Associational Membership and Reputational Influence." Sociological Inquiry 35 (Spring):
176-185.
   This study compared the reputational and positional techniques for measuring power structures.
It was concluded that future studies should continue
to employ both techniques since different results
were found with the use of each technique.

375 Powers, Ronald C. 1967. "Power Actors and Social
Change--Part II." Journal of Cooperative Extension
5 (Winter): 238-248.
   Powers argues that power actors must be able to
understand the decision-making process of the community so that they can be most effective. He
adopted the reputational technique as a tool for community change agents to use in understanding the decision-making process.

376 Preston, James D. 1969. "The Search for Community
Leaders: A Re-examination of the Reputational
Technique." Sociological Inquiry 39 (Winter): 39-
47.
   The Bonjean technique of measuring power was
employed in two southern communities. Generally,
the results supported his technique. Leadership was
general, and all groups of respondents were in general agreement as to the identity of leaders and the
leadership structures. Also, the leadership structures in both communities were highly visible.

377 Smith, Joel, and Thomas Hood. 1966. "The Delinea-
     tion of Community Power Structures by a Reputa-
     tional Approach." Sociological Inquiry 26 (Winter):
     3-14.
        It was concluded that the use of the reputational
     technique employing the nominations of a cross-sec-
     tion of community residents rather than by commu-
     nity leaders will uncover a potential power system.

378 _____, and _____. "The Delineation of Commu-
     nity Power Structures by a Reputational Approach."
     Unpublished paper presented at the meeting of the
     American Sociological Association.

379 Sollie, Carlton, R. 1966. "A Comparison of Reputa-
     tional Techniques for Identifying Leaders." Rural
     Sociology 31 (September): 301-309.
        Four different reputational techniques were used
     to identify community leaders. The four different
     techniques (a panel of experts, community leaders
     identified by the experts, the 'snowball' technique,
     and a random sample of household heads) yielded
     results with a high level of agreement between them.

380 Spiekerman, Ruth Danette Hill. 1968. "Identification
     of Community Power Structure Using the Reputational
     Approach: A Comparative Analysis of Two Texas
     Communities." Unpublished M.S. thesis, Texas.
     A. and M. University.

381 Wolfinger, Raymond E. 1962. "A Plea for a Decent
     Burial." American Sociological Review 26 (Decem-
     ber): 841-847.
        A critique of the reputational technique for mea-
     suring power structures and a plea to end its use
     in future community power research.

382 _____. 1960. "Reputation and Reality in the Study
     of Community Power." American Sociological Review
     25 (October): 636-644.
        A critique of the reputational technique for mea-
     suring power. It was argued that the reputational
     technique should be a first step in studying the struc-
     ture of power in a community. Wolfinger argues
     that it could be used as a guide in uncovering knowl-
     edgeable people in the community who would be used
     to help uncover the total picture of the local power

structure. Detailed analyses of the histories of
actual decisions can best isolate important actors
and important relationships in the community.

POSITIONAL TECHNIQUE

383 Edinger, L. J., and D. D. Searing. 1967. "Social
     Background in Elite Analysis: A Methodological In-
     quiry." American Political Science Review 61 (June):
     428-445.
          The introduction of a multivariate technique for
     use in cross-national comparisons of elite groups.
     This technique permits the investigation and compari-
     son of many relevant variables in social background
     analysis.

384 Schulze, Robert, and Leonard Blumberg. 1957. "The
     Determination of Local Power Elites." American
     Journal of Sociology 63 (November): 290-296.
          Schulze and Blumberg compared two methodological
     tools used in uncovering community power structures;
     the reputational technique and the positional technique.
     They found that the use of these techniques uncover
     different sets of names. They conclude that in any
     study of local power structures both techniques should
     be employed by the researcher.

385 _____, and _____. 1957. "The Selection of Com-
     munity Power Elites." Unpublished paper presented
     at the meeting of the Eastern Sociological Society.

386 Searing, Donald D. 1968. "Rule and Habit: The So-
     cial Background Approach to Elite Analysis." Un-
     published Ph. D. Dissertation, Washington University,
     St. Louis.

387 Singh, Avtar. 1970. "Identifying Community Leaders:
     An Evaluation of the Positional Technique." Unpub-
     lished paper presented at the meeting of the Rural
     Sociological Society.

DECISION-MAKING TECHNIQUE

388 Forward, R. 1969. "Issue Analysis in Community
Power Studies." Australian Journal of Political
History 15 (December): 26-44.

389 Polsby, Nelson W. 1960. How to Study Community
Power: The Pluralist Alternative." Journal of
Politics 22 (August): 474-484.
A 'pluralist alternative' is developed for the study
of community political systems. Polsby recommends
that specific issue-areas be studied, issues should
be important community issues, actual behavior
should be studied, and the outcome of actual decisions should be analyzed.

390 Snyder, Richard C. 1958. "A Decision-Making Approach to the Study of Political Phenomena." In
Approaches to the Study of Politics, edited by
Roland Young. Evanston, Ill.: Northwestern University Press. 3-37.

391 _____, H. W. Bruck, and Burton Sapin. 1956.
"The Decision-Making Approach." In Political Behavior, edited by H. Eulau, S. J. Eldersveld, and
M. Janowitz. Glencoe, Ill.: The Free Press.
352-358.

COMPARATIVE METHODOLOGY

392 Freeman, Linton, Thomas J. Fararo, Warner Bloomberg Jr., and Morris H. O. Sunshine. 1963. "Lo-
cating Leaders in Local Communities: A Comparison
of Some Alternate Approaches." American Sociological Review 28 (October): 791-798.
A comparative approach is used to study the
structure of power in Syracuse, N.Y. Reputation,
participation, social activity, and position were the
methods used. The results were compared and
three leadership groups emerged. The Institutional
Leaders who held formal command over the institutional structure, the Effectors who were the active
workers in community affairs and who were often
the underlings of the Institutional Leaders, and the

> Activists who had no real power base but gained en-
> try into the decision-making process by commitment
> of time and energy.

393 Miller, Delbert C. 1973. "Design Strategies for Comparative International Studies of Community Power."
Social Forces 51 (March): 261-274.

394 _____. 1973. "The Institutional Approach as a
Strategy for Comparative Community Power Structure Studies." In Comparative Community Politics,
edited by Terry N. Clark. Beverly Hills, Cal. :
Sage Publications.

395 _____. 1970. "The Institutional Structure Vs. The
Decision-Making Approach in Comparative Community
Power Structure Studies." Unpublished paper presented at the meeting of the Southwestern Sociological Association.

396 Preston, James D. 1969. "A Comparative Methodology
for Identifying Community Leaders." Rural Sociology
34 (December): 556-562.
    Preston did not find a clear relationship between
identifying techniques and results. All the techniques
he used yielded essentially the same leadership group.
He also found that different techniques do tap different dimensions of leadership.

397 _____. 1969. "The Identification of Community
Power Structures: A Comparative Analysis of Alternative Methodologies." Proceedings of the Southwestern Sociological Association 19 (April): 149-152.

398 _____. 1969. "The Identification of Community
Power Structures: A Comparative Analysis of Alternative Methodologies." Unpublished paper presented
at the meeting of the Southwestern Social Science
Association.

399 Walton, John. 1971. "A Methodology for the Comparative Study of Power: Some Conceptual and Proce-
dural Applications." Social Science Quarterly 53
(June): 39-60.
    Walton suggests four procedures for overcoming
individual biases in community power research.
They are a more specific definition of power, a

comparative framework, specification of the independent and dependent variables, and delineation of the structure of relationships within which power operates.

400 _____. 1970. "A Methodology for the Comparative Study of Power." Unpublished paper presented at the meeting of the Southwestern Sociological Society.

MEASUREMENT OF POWER AND INFLUENCE

401 Brams, Steven J. 1968. "Measuring the Concentration of Power in Political Systems." American Political Science Review 62 (June): 461-475.
Brams developed a quantitative index that measures the degree of concentration of power in a political system.

402 Coleman, James S. 1973. "Loss of Power." American Sociological Review 38 (February): 1-17.

403 Foskett, John M., and Raymond Hohle. 1957. "The Measurement of Influence in Community Affairs." Research Studies of the State College of Washington 25 (June): 148-154.

404 Harsanyi, John. 1962. "Measurement of Social Power in N-Person Reciprocal Power Situations." Behavioral Science 7 (January): 81-91.

405 _____. 1962. "Measurement of Social Power, Opportunity Costs and the Theory of Two Person-Bargaining Games." Behavioral Science 7 (January): 67-80.

406 Jessup, David. 1966. "Potential Power: A Discussion and a New Measure." Berkeley Journal of Sociology 11: 66-81.
A measure of potential power in communities was developed.

407 Levine, Joel L. 1972. "The Sphere of Influence." American Sociological Review 37 (February): 14-27.

408 March, James G. 1956. "Influence Measurement in

Experimental and Semi-Experimental Groups."
Sociometry 19 (December): 260-271.
March argues for caution in the comparative use
of different indices of interpersonal influence.

409   _____. 1955. "An Introduction to the Theory and
Measurement of Influence." American Political
Science Review 49 (June): 431-451.
A formal model of influence and decision-making
was outlined.

410   _____. 1957. "Measurement Concepts in the
Theory of Influence." Journal of Politics 19 (May):
202-226.
March developed measurement concepts dealing
with influence relationships. He distinguished between influence of role qua role and influence of
behavior qua behavior.

411   Rogers, E. M., and D. G. Cartano. 1962. "Methods
of Measuring Opinion Leadership." Public Opinion
Quarterly 26 (Fall): 436-441.

412   Russett, B. M. 1968. "Probabilism and the Number
of Units Affected: Measuring Influence Concentration." American Political Science Review 62 (June):
475-480.
A research note proposing an alternative to
Brams' idea for measuring power concentration.
It is based on the idea of decision-makers influencing other decision-makers rather than on the size
of the domain.

413   Simon, Herbert A. 1953. "Notes on the Observation
and Measurement of Power." Journal of Politics
15 (November): 500-516.
An explication of power and influence and the
bases for the measurement of these two concepts.
Simon suggested the possibility of using notions
from set theory as a basis of measurement.

3

COMMUNITY POWER STUDIES

DISCUSSIONS

352.073
243,3 (1968)

414 Adrian, Charles R. 1961. Governing Urban America.
New York: McGraw-Hill.

415 _____. 1959. "Metropology: Folklore and Field
Research." Public Administration Review 18 (Summer): 208-213.

416 _____, editor. 1960. Social Science and Community Action. East Lansing: Institute for Community
Development and Services, Michigan State University.

01.155
2915

417 Aiken, Michael, and Paul Mott, editors. 1970. The
Structure of Community Power. New York: Random
House.

418 Amendola, G. 1969. "L'Alibi del Potere Locale"
[The Alibi of Local Power]. La Critica Sociologica
11 (August): 105-130.
A review of American research on community
power structure. Amendola found that American
studies have neglected the question of community
values. Amendola hopes that American models can
be adapted for studies in Italy.

52
-72/9

419 American Academy of Political and Social Science.
1967. Governing Urban Society: New Scientific
Approaches. Philadelphia: Monograph No. 7,
American Academy of Political and Social Science.

420 Anderson, William. 1957. "Municipal Government:
No Lost World." American Political Science Re-
view 51 (September): 776-783.
Anderson disagreed with L. J. R. Herson that

the study of municipal government was a 'lost world. '

421 _____. 1955. "Political Influence of the Metropolis."
In The Metropolis in Modern Life, edited by R. M.
Fisher. New York: Doubleday. 57-65.

422 Angell, Robert Cooley. 1951. "The Moral Integration
of American Cities." American Journal of Sociology
42 (July): part II-1-140.

423 Balbo, Laura. 1969. "Struttura del Potere e Processi
di Decisione a Livello di Communitè" [Power Structure and Decision-Making Processes at the Community
Level]. Quaderni di Sociologia 18 (Oct.-Dec.): 466-
494.
A review of community power studies. Balbo
argues that research in this area has not progressed
very far since the basic theoretical and methodological
issues are still debated. Particular attention was
given to studies that emphasized the processes of development, industrialization, and urbanization.

424 Barth, Ernest, and Stuart D. Johnson. 1959. "Community Power and a Typology of Social Issues."
Social Forces 38 (October): 29-32.
It was argued that one failing of researchers has
been the range or type of issues selected in analyz-
ing the structure of power in communities. Barth
and Johnson constructed a five-point typology from
which to pick issues so that a wide range of issues
would be selected. This would insure that a complete picture of the political structure of the community would result.

425 Bonjean, Charles M. 1971. "The Community as Research Site and Object of Inquiry." In Community
Politics: A Behavioral Approach, edited by Charles
M. Bonjean, Terry N. Clark, and Robert L. Lineberry. New York: The Free Press. 5-15.
Bonjean reviews definitions of the concept of community and the classification schemes that social
scientists have used in the study of different communities. Communities have been studied by size, historical development, locations, and economic functions. Functional dimensions of communities that
have emerged from several recent studies were compared and found to be reasonably comparable. Such

functional classifications as Bonjean discusses are
important for establishing major dimensions of differences across communities, for sampling communities for more intensive investigation, and as a
first step toward the development of comparative
propositions.

426 Bonjean, Charles M., Terry N. Clark, and R. L. Lineberry, editors. 1971. Community Politics: A Behavioral
Approach. New York: The Free Press.

427 Brookes, R. H. 1963. "Politics and Administration in
Local Government." New Zealand Journal of Public
Administration 26 (September): 9-18.

428 Cho, Yong H. 1967. "The Effect of Local Government
Systems on Local Policy Outcomes in the United
States." Public Administration Review 27 (March):
31-39.

429 Churchward, L. G. 1959. "Soviet Local Government."
Australian Outlook 13 (September): 211-222.

430 Clark, Terry N. 1967. "Power and Community Structure: Who Governs, Where and When?" Sociological
Quarterly 8 (Summer): 291-316.
    An inventory of propositions was presented divided
into basic demographic variables, adaptation variables,
goal attainment variables, integration variables, and
latent pattern-maintenance and tension management
variables. Their relationships to community power
structures were explored.

431 Connery, Robert H., and Demetrios Caraley, editors.
1969. Governing the City: Challenges and Options
for New York. New York: Praeger.

432 Dahl, Robert. 1960. "The Analysis of Influence in
Local Communities." In Social Science and Commu-
nity Action, edited by Charles Adrian. East Lansing:
Michigan State University Press. 25-42.

433 D'Antonio, William V. and H. J. Ehrlich, editors.
1961. Power and Democracy in America. Notre
Dame, Ind.: University of Notre Dame Press.

434 Dye, Thomas. 1965. "City-Suburban Social Distance

and Public Policy." Social Forces 44 (September):
100-106.

The differences in the character of the city and
suburbs produce identifiable differences in public
policy choices. Suburbanites spend more on education but less on municipal services than do city residents. The taxes in the suburbs are lower because
of the cut in services over the city.

321.8
P887p

435 Ehrlich, Howard. 1961. "Power and Democracy: A
Critical Discussion." In Power and Democracy in
America, edited by William V. D'Antonio and Howard
Ehrlich. Notre Dame, Ind.: University of Notre
Dame Press. 91-123.

O

436 Gamson, William A. 1961. "Some Dimensions of Community Power." Unpublished paper presented at the
meeting of the American Sociological Association.

352.0748
G464g

437 Gilbert, Charles. 1967. Governing the Suburbs.
Bloomington: Indiana University Press.

O

438 Goldstein, Marshall N. 1962. "Absentee Ownership
and Monolithic Power Structures: Two Questions for
Community Studies." In Current Trends in Comparative Community Studies, edited by Bert Swanson.
Kansas City, Mo.: Community Studies, Inc. 49-59.

O

439 Greenstein, Fred I. 1964. "The Changing Pattern of
Urban Party Politics." The Annals of the American
Academy of Political and Social Science 353 (May):
1-13.

Greenstein speculates about the future of old-style
party politics. If the cities become basically com-
posed of lower-class non-white people, old-style
politics, with political machines playing important
roles, is likely to continue.

352.073
G816m

440 Greer, Scott. 1963. Metropolitics: A Study of Political Culture. New York: John Wiley.

O

441 _____. 1960. "The Social Structure and Political
Process of Suburbia." American Sociological Review
25 (August): 514-526.

A typology of the socio-political structure of suburbia was developed. Local community actors' involvement in local political affairs was also examined.

442 Hawley, Ames H., and Basil G. Zimmer. 1970. The
Metropolitan Community: Its People and Government. Beverly Hills, Cal.: Sage Publications.

443 Hawley, Willis, and Frederick M. Wirt, editors. 1968.
The Search for Community Power. Englewood
Cliffs, N. J.: Prentice-Hall.

444 Hays, Forbes B. 1965. Community Leadership:. The
Regional Plan Association of New York. New York:
Columbia University Press.

445 Hencley, Stephen P. 1964. "The Study of Community
Politics and Power." In The Politics of Education
in the Local Community, edited by Robert S. Cahill
and Stephen Hencley. Danville, Ill.: Interstate
Printers & Publishers. 5-26.

446 Herson, Lawrence J. R. 1957. "The Lost World of
Municipal Government." American Political Science
Review 51 (June): 330-345.
A close examination of the leading trends in the
municipal government. An explanation of the short-
comings of this form of government with suggestions
for its future was also examined.

447 Holden, Matthew, Jr. 1964. "The Governance of the
Metropolis as a Problem of Diplomacy." Journal
of Politics 26 (August): 627-647.
Metropolitan politics and international politics can
be studied within a common frame of reference--
diplomacy. Diplomatic systems are ecological communities with governmental actors as the primary
participants and a mythology that governmental actors
are the only legitimate actors. International relations theory can be applied to the study of metropolitan consensus formation.

448 Horowitz, Irving Lois. 1966. "La Politica Urbana en
Latinoamerica" [Urban Politics in Latin America].
Revista Mexicana de Sociologia 28 (Jan.-Mar.): 71-
111.
Horowitz found that political power was concentrated in the big cities in Latin America. This was
due to the concentration of the upper-classes in
these areas.

449   Janowitz, Morris, editor. 1961. Community Political
      Systems. Glencoe, Ill.: The Free Press.

450   Kammerer, Gladys M. 1963. "The Politics of Metrop-
      olis: Still a Frontier." Public Administration Re-
      view 23 (December): 240-246.

352.0713
K17u
451   Kaplan, Harold. 1967. Urban Political Systems. New
      York: Columbia University Press.

452   Kaufman, Herbert. 1958. "The Next Step in Case
      Studies." Public Administration Review 18 (Winter):
      52-59.

453   Knill, William D. 1964. "Community Decision Pro-
      cesses: Research Strategies." In The Politics of
      Education in the Local Community, edited by Robert
      S. Cahill and Stephen Hencley. Danville, Ill.:
      Interstate Printers & Publishers. 77-92.

352.073
K87n
454   Kotler, Milton. 1969. Neighborhood Government: The
      Local Foundations of Political Life. Indianapolis:
      Bobbs-Merrill.

455   Liebman, C. S. 1961. "Electorates Interest Groups
      and Local Government Policy." American Behav-
      ioral Scientist 4 (January): 9-11.

456   Lindbolm, C. E. 1959. "The Science of 'Muddling
      Through'." Public Administration Review 19 (Spring):
      79-88.

457   Lineberry, Robert L. 1971. "Approaches to the Study
      of Community Politics." In Community Politics: A
      Behavioral Approach, edited by Charles M. Bonjean,
      Terry N. Clark, and Robert L. Lineberry. New
      York: The Free Press. 16-25.
          Lineberry focused on two approaches to the study
      of community politics: micro and macro approaches.
      Macro-analysis of communities refers to the study of
      the properties of communities, while micro-level
      analysis refers to the study of sub-community levels.
      To a great degree, Lineberry argues, work has
      tended to advance independently on each of these
      levels.   More effort is necessary to integrate re-
      search on the two levels.

458 _____, and Edmund P. Fowler. 1967. "Reformism
and Public Policies in American Cities." Americaⁿ
Political Science Review 61 (September): 701-716.

Using a national sample of American cities, Lineberry and Fowler examined the impact of the so-
called reform characteristics (city-manager, nonpartisan elections, at-large constituencies) on policy
outputs. They found that cities with reform characteristics tended to be 'less responsive' to their popu-
lations. That is, they correlated several city population characteristics with policy outputs (budgetary
activities and tax levels). When they compared the
correlations in cities with reform and unreformed
characteristics, they found higher correlations in the
unreformed cities. They concluded that reform characteristics, as Banfield and Wilson and others had
argued earlier, tended to isolate the city manager
and other leading decision-makers from citizen
opinion--at least as compared with non-reformed
cities.

459 Lineberry, Robert L., and Ira Sharkansky. 1971. Urban Politics
and Public Policy. New York: Harper & Row.

460 Long, Norton E. 1957. "Aristotle and the Study of
Local Government." Social Research 24 (Autumn):
287-310.

461 _____. 1959. "The Corporation, Its Satellites and
the Local Community." In Corporation in Modern
Society, edited by E. S. Mason. Cambridge, Mass.:
Harvard University Press. 202-217.

462 _____. 1958. "The Local Community as an Ecology
of Games." American Journal of Sociology 64 (November): 251-261.

The community is seen as a set of games with
the community residents playing the roles in the
games. Although most of the players are unaware
of it, they support the functional balance and ecology
of the community by fulfilling their roles in the
games.

463 _____. 1961. "Sayre and Kaufman's New York:
Competition Without Chaos." Public Administration
Review 21 (Summer): 23-30.

464 _____. 1962. "Some Observations Toward a Natural History of Metropolitan Politics." In The Polity by Norton Long, edited by Charles Press. Chicago: Rand McNally. 196-214.

465 Lowi, Theodore J. 1967. "Machine Politics--Old and New." The Public Interest 9 (Fall): 83-92.

466 Lowry, Ritchie P. 1963. "The Myth and Reality of Grass-Roots Democracy." International Review of Community Development 11: 3-16.

467 Martin-Retortillo Baquer, S. 1964. "Presupuestos Politicos del Regimen Local" [Political Assumptions of Local Government]. Revista de Administración Publica 43 (Janv.-Apvr.): 9-35.

468 Michetti, H. H., and M. A. de A. G. Parahyba. 1968. "O Jogo das Forças Politicas na Vids de Araraquara" [The Interplay of Political Forces in the Life of Araraquara]. Ciencias Politicas y Sociales 2 (Juil.-Sept.): 59-78.

469 Minar, David W. 1964. "Community Characteristics, Conflict and Power Structures." In The Politics of Education in the Local Community, edited by Robert S. Cahill and Stephen Hencley. Danville, Ill.: Interstate Printers & Publishers. 125-144.

470 Monti, Daniel. 1973. "Community Power and Collective Violence." Unpublished paper presented at the meeting of the American Sociological Association.

471 Montiminy, Jean-Paul. 1966. "Les Grands Thêmes de l'Etude du Pouvoir au Quebec" [The Great Themes of the Study of Power in Quebec]. Recherches Sociographiques 7 (Jan.-Aug.): 245-250.
     A discussion of the multiple aspects of power in French Canada. Questions are raised for future research to distinguish political power from other forms of power.

472 Mott, Paul E. 1970. "The Role of the Absentee-Owned Corporation in the Changing Community." In The Structure of Community Power, edited by Paul Mott and Michael Aiken. New York: Random House. 170-179.

473 Palmer, Norman D. 1967. "Lokalne Systemy Polit-
     yczne w Poludniowei Asji: Eksperymenty w 'Demo-
     kratycznei Decentralizacji' " [Local Political Systems
     in South Asia: Experiments in 'Democratic Decen-
     tralization']. Studia Socjologiczno Polityczne 23:
     125-141.

474 Polsby, Nelson W. 1960. "Power in Middletown:
     Fact and Value in Community Research." The
     Canadian Journal of Economics and Political Science
     26 (November): 592-603.

475 _____. 1959. "The Sociology of Community Power:
     A Reassessment." Social Forces 37 (March): 232-
     236.
          Polsby argues for more studies dealing with de-
     cision-making processes of communities rather than
     the examination of reputations, attributions and inten-
     tions.

476 _____. 1959. "Three Problems in the Analysis of
     Community Power." American Sociological Review
     24 (December): 796-803.
          The problems of the identification of leaders, the
     definition of the power structure, and the relation-
     ships between the economic, status, and power elites
     are examined. It was found that there was not a
     significant overlap of leaders across issue areas.

477 Reader, A., and Michael N. Danielson, editors. 1966.
     Metropolitan Politics. Boston: Little, Brown.

478 Richardson, B. M. 1967. "Japanese Local Politics:
     Support Mobilization and Leadership Styles." Asian
     Survey 7 (December): 860-875.

479 Riedel, James A., editor. 1971. New Perspective on
     State and Local Politics. Waltham, Mass.: Blaisdell
     Pub. Co.

480 Riker, William H. 1959. The Study of Local Politics.
     New York: Random House.

481 Rose, Arnold M. 1967. "Issues in the Study of Local
     Community Power." In The Power Structure: Polit-
     ical Process in American Society, by Arnold Rose.
     New York: Oxford University Press. 255-297.

482 _____. 1967. "Perceptions of Power and Influence."
In The Power Structure: Political Process in Ameri-
can Society, by Arnold Rose. New York: Oxford
University Press. 298-355.

483 Rosenthal, Donald B. 1970. "Deurbanization, Elite
Displacement and Political Change in India." Comparative Politics 2 (January): 169-201.

484 _____. 1968. "Deurbanization, Elite Displacement
and Political Change in India." Unpublished paper
presented at the meeting of the American Political
Science Association.

485 Rossi, Peter H. 1961. "Power and Politics: A Road
to Social Reform." Social Science Review 35 (December): 359-369.
      Rossi argues that politicians need people to vali-
date the programs that they present. He also argues
that it would be possible for the social worker to
fill the now vacant staff role of a generator of ideology.

486 _____. 1961. "What Makes Communities Tick?"
Unpublished paper presented at the meeting of the
National Advisory Committee on Local Health De-
partments, National Opinion Research Center, University of Chicago.

487 _____, and Alice S. Rossi. 1956. "An Historical
Perspective on the Function of Local Politics." Un-
published paper presented at the meeting of the
American Sociological Society.

488 Rudolph, Lloyd I. 1961. "Urban Life and Populist
Radicalism." Journal of Asian Studies 20 (February):
283-297.

489 Salisbury, Robert H. 1964. "Urban Politics: The New
Convergence of Power." Journal of Politics 26
(November): 775-797.
      Salisbury found that the central role in urban poli-
tics is played by the elected political leadership.

490 _____. 1963. "Urban Politics: The New Convergence of Power." Unpublished paper presented at
the meeting of the American Political Science Association.

491   Sharpe, L. J.   1960.   "The Politics of Local Government in Greater London."   Public Administration 38
(Summer):   157-172.

492   Smith, T. D.   1965.   "Local Government in Newcastle-
Upon-Tyne: The Background to Some Recent Developments."   Public Administration 43 (Winter):   413-
417.

493   Spinrad, William.   1965.   "Power in Local Communities."
Social Problems 12 (Winter):   335-356.
        Spinrad found community power structures to be rela-
tively pluralistic depending on the type of community
issue that was investigated.   He also found the communities' rejection of a heavy reliance on the business
elite for the formal political structure.

494   Tinker, H.   1960.   "Authority and Community in Village
India."   Journal of African Administration 12 (October):   193-210.

495   Vanecko, James J.   1969.   "Community Mobilization
and Institutional Change: The Influence of the Community Action Program in Large Cities."   Social
Science Quarterly 50 (December):   609-630.

496   Warren, Roland L.   1956.   "Toward a Typology of
Extra-Community Controls Limiting Local Community
Autonomy."   Social Forces 34 (May):   339-341.
        A study of the extra-community controls that tend
to limit or help to control the amount of autonomy
that a community can have.   While community studies
often held that communities were autonomous, the
data often suggest that this was not the case.

497   Westby, David L.   1966.   "The Civic Sphere in the
American City."   Social Forces 65 (December):   161-
170.
        Through a bifurcation of the city into political and
civic leadership spheres, the civic status sphere has
emerged as being higher than the political status
sphere.

498   Whalen, Hugh.   1960.   "Ideology, Democracy, and the
Foundations of Local Self-Government."   Canadian
Journal of Economics and Political Science 26
(August):   377-395.

499 Wilkinson, Kenneth P.   1970.   "Phases and Roles in
        Community Action."   Rural Sociology 35 (March):
        54-68.
            A context for the analysis of community action
        roles was formulated by a conceptualization of the
        community in interactional terms.

500 Williams, Oliver P.   1967.   "Life Style Values and
        Political Decentralization in Metropolitan Areas."
        Southwestern Social Science Quarterly 48 (December):
        299-310.

501 _____, and Charles Press, editors.   1969.   Democ-
        racy in Urban America.   Chicago: Rand McNally &
        Company.

502 Wilson, James Q. , editor.   1968.   City Politics and
        Public Policy.   New York: John Wiley and Sons.

503 Wirt, Frederick M.   1965.   "The Political Sociology
        of American Suburbia: A Reinterpretation."   Journal
        of Politics 27 (August):   647-666.
            Wirt argues that patterns of politics and political
        values are similar in the cities and suburbs.

504 Wood, Robert C.   1958.   Suburbia: Its People and
        Their Politics.   Boston: Houghton Mifflin Company.

505 Worsley, Peter.   1964.   "The Distribution of Power in
        Industrial Society."   Sociological Review Monograph
        8 (October):   15-41.

506 Wrong, Dennis.   1963.   "Who Runs American Cities?"
        New Society 1 (April):   16-17.

507 Yager, John W.   1963.   "Who Runs Our Town?"   Na-
        tional Civic Review 52 (May):   255-259.

GENERAL STUDIES

508 Abu-Laban, Baha.   1967.   "Social Change and Local
        Politics: The Case of Sidon, Lebanon."   Unpublished
        paper presented at the meeting of the American
        Sociological Association.

509 Agger, Robert and Vincent Ostrom. 1956. "The Polit-
     ical Structure of a Small Community." Public Opin-
     ion Quarterly 20 (Spring): 81-89.

510 Akimoto, Ritsuo. 1964. "Sangyotoshi ni Okeru Kenryo-
     kukozo" [Power Structure in Industrial City]. Shakai-
     kagaku Tokyu 9 (March): 55-94.

511 Allen, C. H. 1960. "Local Government and Political
     Consciousness in the British Solomon Islands Pro-
     tectorate." Journal of African Administration 12
     (July): 158-163.

512 Ashraf, Ali. 1966. The City Government of Calcutta:
     A Study of Inertia. New York: Asia Publishing
     House.

513 Auerbach, Arnold J. 1965. "Power and Progress in
     Pittsburgh." Transaction 2 (Sept. /Oct.): 15-20.

514 Bailey, Norman A. 1968. "Local and Community
     Power in Angola." Western Political Quarterly 21
     (September): 400-408.

515 Balbo, Laura. 1969. "Perception of Community Issues
     and Political Demand: A Study of Decision-Making in
     a Southern Italian Community." Unpublished paper
     presented at the meeting of the International Confer-
     ence on Community Decision-Making, Milan.

516 Baltzell, Edward Digby. 1958. Philadelphia Gentlemen:
     The Making of a National Upper Class. Glencoe,
     Ill.: The Free Press.

517 Banfield, Edward C. 1961. Political Influence: A New
     Theory of Urban Politics. Glencoe, Ill.: The Free
     Press.
         Seven case studies of the decision-making process
     in Chicago. Banfield found the most important in-
     fluentials to be heads of large organizations, the
     civic leaders and the formal elected officials. There
     was an absence of 'top leadership'. Here Banfield
     developed his clearest analysis of the political ma-
     chine in Chicago. It functioned to centralize power
     in the Democratic Party in such a manner that the
     dispersion of legal authority could be overcome.
     Fragmentation that was characteristic of New York

or Los Angeles was thus much less a barrier to effective decision-making in Chicago.

518   Barlow, Henry M.   1968.   "Community Power Structure
      and Decision Making in an Urban Community." Un-
      published Ph. D. dissertation, The Ohio State Univer-
      sity.
          The power structure of a medium-sized metropolis
      was examined.   It was found that four coalitions were
      dominant in community politics.   Barlow also found
      that there was a conflict between the coalitions, es-
      pecially the conservative and progressive ones.

519   Bartholomew, David K.   1971.   "An Analysis of Change
      in the Power System and Decision-Making Process
      in a Selected County." Unpublished Ed. D. disserta-
      tion, University of Florida.
          Bartholomew found three key factors which con-
      tributed to the lack of social change in the county;
      power resources controlled by a small group, an un-
      diversified economy, and a stable population.

520   Belknap, George M. and Ralph Smuckler.   1956.   "Po-
      litical Power Relations in a Mid-West City." Public
      Opinion Quarterly 20 (Spring): 73-81.
          A small group of 'top leaders' were found to be
      instrumental in many of the important decisions in
      the community.   A group underneath this top group
      also exerted some influence in community politics.
      A pyramidal model of power was found.

521   Birch, A. H.   1959.   Small-Town Politics: A Study of
      Political Life in Glossop.   New York: Oxford Uni-
      versity Press.

522   Bittinger, Beau S.   1967.   "Leadership Systems and
      Social Change in a Texas City of 100,000." Un-
      published Ph. D. dissertation, University of Texas.

523   Blaiser, Cole.   1966.   "Power and Social Change in
      Colombia: The Cauca Valley." Journal of Inter-
      American Studies 8 (July): 386-410.

524   Bloomberg, Warner, Jr.   1960.   "The Structure of
      Power in Stackton.   Unpublished Ph. D. dissertation,
      University of Chicago.

525 Blumberg, Leonard U. 1955. "Community Leaders:
     The Social Bases and Social Psychological Concom-
     mitants of Community Power." Unpublished Ph. D.
     dissertation, University of Michigan.

526 Boissevain, J. 1962. "Maltese Village Politics and
     Their Relation to National Politics." Journal of
     Commonwealth Political Studies 1 (November): 211-
     222.

527 Booth, David A. 1963. Metropolitics: The Nashville
     Consolidation. East Lansing: Institute for Commu-
     nity Development and Services, Michigan State Uni-
     versity.
         The key leaders in Nashville were split on the
     issue of consolidation. They did little campaigning
     for it either way. The top leadership group was
     dominated by four officeholders.

528 _____, and Charles R. Adrian. 1963. "Elections
     and Community Power." Journal of Politics 25
     (February): 107-118.
         A study of a conservative city found that it was
     possible for a newcomer to the city to be elected to
     political office. Booth and Adrian argue that the
     community power structure of other comparable
     cities may not be as solid and stable as has been
     hypothesized.

529 _____, and Charles R. Adrian. 1962. "Power
     Structure and Community Change: A Replication
     Study of Community A." Midwest Journal of Polit-
     ical Science 6 (August): 277-296.

530 Bouma, Donald H. 1970. "The Issue-Analysis Ap-
     proach to Community Power: A Case Study of
     Realtors in Kalamazoo." American Journal of
     Economics and Sociology 29 (July): 241-252.
         The voters of Kalamazoo defeated a housing pro-
     posal because the realtors in the community opposed
     it. This brings into question the validity of the rep-
     utational technique since the community residents
     that were questioned generally did not identify the
     real estate board members as major influentials in
     Kalamazoo.

531 Brand, J. A. 1971. "The Politics of Fluoridation:

A Community Conflict." <u>Political Studies</u> 19 (December): 430-439.

532 Brier, A. P. 1970. "The Decision Process in Local
     Government: A Case Study of Fluoridation in Hull."
     <u>Public Administration</u> 48 (Summer): 153-168.

533 Caplow, Theodore, Sheldon Stryker, and Samuel E.
     Wallace. 1964. <u>The Urban Ambience: A Study of
     San Juan, Puerto Rico</u>. Totowa, N. J.: Bedminster
     Press.

534 Cargan, Leonard. 1968. "Community Power in a Dormitory City." Unpublished Ph.D. dissertation,
     Wayne State University.

535 Carney, Francis M. 1964. "The Decentralized Politics of Los Angeles." <u>The Annals of the American
     Academy of Political and Social Science</u> 353 (May):
     107-121.
          Despite rising opposition, the people of Los
     Angeles seemed content to continue with decentralized
     politics because it allowed the city to remain unbossed
     and scandal-free.

536 Carpenter, Dwight M. 1964. "The Trend Towards
     Metropolitan Government in Wichita: A Case Study
     of Local Decision-Making." Unpublished Ph.D. dissertation, University of Illinois.
          A study of the trend toward area-wide government
     and the actions of the decision-making structure in
     Wichita. Carpenter argues that city-county consolidation would be the best solution to the problem of
     government in the Wichita area.

537 Carrere, Thomas A. 1971. "A Study of the Power
     Structure of a Selected South Carolina County." Unpublished Ph.D. dissertation, University of South
     Carolina.

538 Cattell, David T. 1964. "Leningrad: A Case Study of
     Soviet Local Government." <u>Western Political Quarterly</u> 17 (June): 188-199.

539 _____. 1968. <u>Leningrad: A Case Study of Soviet
     Urban Government</u>. New York: Praeger.

540 Clauss, William A. 1970. "An Analytical Look at the
     Black, the White and the Overall Power Structures
     of a Selected County in Florida." Unpublished Ph. D.
     dissertation, University of Miami.

541 Clelland, Donald A. 1962. "Economic Dominance and
     Community Power in a Middle-Sized City." Unpub-
     lished paper presented at the meeting of the Ohio
     Valley Sociological Society.

542 Codding, G. A., Jr. 1967. Governing the Commune
     of Veyrier: Politics in Swiss Local Government.
     Boulder: University of Colorado Press.

543 Coleman, James S. 1957. Community Conflict. Glen-
     coe, Ill.: The Free Press.

544 Coutler, Phillip B. 1966. "The Urban Political Elite:
     Power and Decision-Making in Schenectady." Unpub-
     lished Ph. D. dissertation, State University of New
     York, Albany.

545 Crain, Robert L., and Donald B. Rosenthal. 1967.
     "Community Status as a Dimension of Local Decision-
     Making." American Sociological Review 32 (Decem-
     ber): 970-984.
        Crain and Rosenthal found support for their hy-
     pothesis that a well educated population can immo-
     bilize the government from exercising its decision-
     making powers by high levels of citizen participation.

546 Cuyugan, Ruben Dario Santos. 1959. "Decision-Makers
     in a New England Community: A Study of Social In-
     fluence and Social Power." Unpublished Ph. D. dis-
     sertation, Harvard University.

547 Dahl, Robert A. 1958. "Organization for Decisions in
     New Haven." Unpublished paper presented at the
     meeting of the American Political Science Associa-
     tion.

548 _____. 1961. Who Governs? Democracy and
     Power in an American City. New Haven, Conn.:
     Yale University Press.
        The classic study of the structure of power and
     influence in New Haven. This study was undertaken

as an answer to Hunter's study of Atlanta. Basic
concepts elaborated in this study were pluralism,
resources, slack, issue areas, and the decisional
approach to studying influence. Dahl was concerned
theoretically that different actors exercised influence
in different areas. To ascertain the degree to which
such a pluralist pattern of influence was in fact present, he studied three issue areas in depth: urban renewal, the election of mayors, and public education.
The decisional approach was used, in which inter-
views, analyses of newspaper accounts, attendance
at meetings, and similar procedures were combined
to reconstruct the details of basic decisions in each
of the three issue areas. The overlap of actors
across issue areas was then computed, and only the
political actors (mainly the mayor) were found to be
consistently important across issue areas. Active
participants were also classified in terms of occupa-
tion and social status, and they were found infre-
quently to be major business leaders or of high social status. The mechanisms of indirect control of
elected officials by the electorate were carefully
analyzed. Although few actors were central in certain decisions, it was pointed out that when a decision runs counter to the basic concerns of community
residents, it is likely that they will begin to activate
their resources and that the slack in the political
system will decrease.

549 Davis, M. 1959-1960. "Community Attitudes Towards
     Fluoridation." Public Opinion Quarterly 23 (Winter):
     474-482.

550 _____. 1967. "Some Aspects of Detroit's Decisional
     Profile." Administrative Science Quarterly 12
     (September): 209-224.

551 Dirks, Robert. 1971. "Local-Level Politics in Rum
     Bay, Tortola." Unpublished Ph.D. Dissertation,
     Case Western Reserve University.

552 Dye, Thomas. 1962. "Popular Images of Decision-
     Making in Suburban Communities." Sociology and
     Social Research 47 (October): 75-83.
        This study of the perception of the power struc-
     ture by suburban residents found that they believed
     that a small group of decision-makers was

instrumental in the resolution of most community issues. Public officials disagreed with the residents
and did not believe that a small group was instrumental in community decision-making.

553 Edgar, Richard E.   1970.   Urban Power and Social
     Welfare: Corporate Influence in an American City.
     Beverly Hills, Cal.: Sage Publications.

554 Edwards, H. T.   1967.   "Power Structure and Its
     Communication Behavior in San Jose, Costa Rica."
     Journal of Inter-American Studies 9 (April): 236-
     247.

555 Ewen, Lynda Ann.   1971.   "Who Rules Detroit?"   Un-
     published paper at the meeting of the American
     Sociological Association.

556 Frederickson, M. George, and Linda Schluter O'Leary.
     1973.   Power, Public Opinion, and Policy in a
     Metropolitan Community: A Case Study of Syracuse,
     New York. New York: Praeger.

557 Freeman, Linton C.   1968.   Patterns of Local Commu-
     nity Leadership. Indianapolis: Bobbs-Merrill.
         Freeman agrees with Martin et al. that the power
     structure of Syracuse has become more decentralized
     than in the 1930's. Freeman reached his conclusions
     by examining patterns of participation by individuals
     and organizations.

558 _____, Warner Bloomberg Jr., Stephen Koff, Morris
     H. Sunshine, and Thomas J. Fararo.   1960.   Local
     Community Leadership. Syracuse, N.Y.: University
     College of Syracuse University.

559 _____, Thomas J. Fararo, Warner Bloomberg Jr.,
     and Morris H. Sunshine.   1962.   Metropolitan De-
     cision-Making: Further Analyses From the Syracuse
     Study of Local Community Leadership. Syracuse,
     N.Y.: University College of Syracuse University.

560 French, Robert Mills.   1968.   "Change Comes to
     Cornucopia--Industry and the Community." In The
     Community: A Comparative Perspective, edited by
     Robert Mills French. Itasca, Ill.: F. E. Peacock.
     392-407.

Cornucopia's power structure changed over the years from pyramidal to factional to pluralistic. The control of the economy was the key determining factor in the type of power structure in Cornucopia. As absentee-ownership of industry increased, the socio-political and socio-economic spheres fell into the hands of local leaders.

561 _____. 1967. "Cornucopia in Transition." Unpublished Ph. D. dissertation, University of Wisconsin.

562 _____. 1970. "Economic Change and Community Power Structure: Transition in Cornucopia." In The Structure of Community Power, edited by Michael Aiken and Paul Mott. New York: Random House. 180-189.

563 _____. 1969. "Economic Change and Community Power Structure: Transition in Cornucopia." Unpublished paper presented at the meeting of the American Sociological Association.

564 _____, and Michael Aiken. 1968. "Community Power in Cornucopia: A Replication in a Small Community of the Bonjean Technique of Identifying Community Leaders." Sociological Quarterly 9 (Spring): 261-270.

French and Aiken's findings were quite similar to the findings of Bonjean, Miller, and Dirksen. French and Aiken also found that the top reputational leadership were more aware of the decision-making process than other community residents.

565 Frolic, B. Michael. 1972. "Decision-Making in Soviet Cities." American Political Science Review 66 (March): 38-52.

566 _____. 1970. "Soviet Urban Politics." Unpublished Ph. D. dissertation, Cornell University.

567 Gamberg, Herbert. 1969. The Escape From Power: Politics in an American Community. Monticello, Ill.: Exchange Bibliography No. 106, Council of Planning Librarians.

568 Gamson, William A. 1965. "Community Issues and Their Outcome: How to Lose a Fluoridation

Referendum." In <u>Applied Sociology: Opportunities and Problems</u>, edited by Alvin Gouldner and S. M. Miller. New York: The Free Press. 350-357.

569 Garvelink, Roger H. 1970. "A Study of Citizens Committees: The Relationship of the Positions in the Community Power Structure of the Citizens Serving as Members of Citizens and the Citizens Advocating the Use of Citizens Committees." Unpublished Ph. D. dissertation, University of Michigan.

570 Gereffi, Gary Allen. 1970. "Dimensions of Community Power: A Study of an Unincorporated Town." <u>Sociological Focus</u> 3 (Summer): 43-64.
    Four different measurement techniques were used to uncover the leadership structure of the community. There was an overlapping group of leaders found from the use of these techniques. Gereffi concluded that for future community power studies to be useful, the researcher must employ multiple techniques in his research.

571 Gettel, Gerhard Frederick. 1956. "A Study of Power in a North Central State Community." Unpublished Ph. D. dissertation, Michigan State University.

572 Gordon, Chad. 1966. "Decision-Making Processes in the Cambridge NASA Proposal." Unpublished paper presented at the meeting of the Eastern Sociological Society.

573 Gore, William J. and Robert L. Peabody. 1958. "The Functions of the Political Campaign." <u>Western Political Quarterly</u> 11 (March): 55-70.

574 Gourley, Harold V. 1962. "Patterns of Leadership in Decision Making in a Selected County." Unpublished Ed. D. dissertation, University of Florida.

575 Grant, Daniel R. 1964. "Metropolitics and Professional Political Leadership: The Case of Nashville." <u>The Annals of the American Academy of Political and Social Science</u> 353 (May): 72-83.
    Grant argues that the participation of professional political leaders does not necessarily destroy possibilities of metropolitan reform.

576   _____. 1955. "Urban and Suburban Nashville: A
       Case Study in Metropolitanism." Journal of Politics
       17 (February): 82-99.

577   Gravel, Pierre Bettez. 1962. "The Play for Power:
       Description of a Community in Eastern Ruanda."
       Unpublished Ph. D. dissertation, University of
       Michigan.

578   Green, B. S. R. 1968. "Community Decision-Making
       in a Georgian City." Unpublished Ph. D. disserta-
       tion, Bath University of Technology.

579   Greer, Ann Lennarson. 1971. "David and Goliath:
       The Mayor and the Economic Elite." Unpublished
       paper presented at the meeting of the American
       Sociological Association.

580   _____. 1970. "The Mayor's Mandate: A Study of
       Political Integration." Unpublished Ph. D. disserta-
       tion, Northwestern University.

581   _____. 1971. "Setting the Civic Agenda: The
       Role of the Strong Mayor." Unpublished paper pre-
       sented at the meeting of the Society for the Study
       of Social Problems.

582   Hammack, David C. 1972. "Implications of Historical
       Knowledge for Theories of Community Power: Par-
       ticipation in Major Decisions in New York City Dur-
       ing the 1890's." Unpublished paper presented at the
       meeting of the American Sociological Association.

583   Hampton, William. 1970. Democracy and Community:
       A Study of Politics in Scheffield. New York: Oxford
       University Press.

584   Hanson, Robert C. 1959. "Predicting a Community
       Decision: A Test of the Miller-Form Theory."
       American Sociological Review 24 (October): 662-
       671.
            Hanson's data supports the Miller-Form theory of
       issue outcome in community decision-making.

585   Hart, Henry C. 1961. "Bombay Politics: Pluralism
       or Polarization?" Journal of Asian Studies 20
       (February): 267-274.

586 _____. 1960. "Urban Politics in Bombay: The
Meaning of Community." Economic Weekly 12 (June):
983-988.

587 Hautaluoma, J., R. Loomis, and W. Viney. 1970.
"Organizational Influence in Denver: Structure and
Process." Rocky Mountain Social Science Journal 7
(October): 11-16.
Thirty-four knowledgeable informants were asked
to rate ten organizations and their influence on the
outcome of four key community issues. They found
that businessmen were the most influential community
group. The informants indicated that economic status and achievement were the main attributes of a
community influential.

588 Hawkins, Brett W. 1967. "Life Style, Demographic
Distance and Voter Support of City-County Consolida-
tion." Southwestern Social Science Quarterly 48
(December): 325-337.
Impact of life-style differences did not appear to
be a major obstacle to the complete consolidation of
American cities.

589 _____. 1966. Nashville Metro. Nashville, Tenn.:
Vanderbilt University Press.

590 Hayes, Edward C. 1969. "Power Structure and the
Urban Crisis: Oakland, California." Unpublished
Ph.D. dissertation, University of California,
Berkeley.

591 _____. 1972. Power Structure and Urban Policy:
Who Rules in Oakland? New York: McGraw-Hill.

592 Hoffer, Charles R. and Walter Freeman. 1955. Social
Action Resulting From Industrial Development. East
Lansing: Michigan State University, Agriculture Ex-
periment Station, Special Bulletin 401.

593 Hoffman, Daniel. 1971. "The Power Elite in Chicago."
Unpublished paper presented at the meeting of the
American Sociological Association.

594 Holden, Matthew, Jr. 1961. "Decision-Making on a
Metropolitan Government Proposition: The Case of
Cuyahoga County, Ohio, 1958-1959." Unpublished

Ph. D. dissertation, Northwestern University.

595   Hollingshead, A. B.   1949.   Elmtown's Youth.   New
        York: John Wiley & Sons.
             Through the youth of Elmtown, Hollingshead ex-
        amined the prestige system of the community and
        how the various social classes influenced community
        decisions.

596   Hoskin, Gary.   1967.   "Community Power and Political
        Modernization: A Study of a Venezuelan City."   Un-
        published Ph. D. dissertation, University of Illinois.

597   _____.   1968.   "Power Structure in a Venezuelan
        Town: The Case of San Cristobal."   International
        Journal of Comparative Sociology 9 (September-
        December):   188-207.
             A study of the power structure of San Cristobal,
        Venezuela.   The reputational and decision-making
        techniques for identifying community leaders were
        used and the power structure of San Cristobal was
        found to be transitory rather than stable lending sup-
        port to the pluralist theses of shifting power from
        issue to issue.

598   _____.   1967.   "Power Structure in a Venezuelan
        Town: The Case of San Cristobal."   Unpublished
        paper presented at the annual meeting of the Ameri-
        can Sociological Association.

599   Hunter, Floyd.   1953.   Community Power Structure.
        Chapel Hill: University of North Carolina Press.
             The pioneer study of community power structure.
        A study of Atlanta, Georgia, in which Hunter found
        a small group of leaders controlling most of the
        major community decisions.   Hunter developed and
        used the reputational technique for identifying com-
        munity leaders in this study.

600   _____.   1964.   Housing Discrimination in Oakland,
        California.   Oakland, Cal. :   A Study Prepared for
        the Mayor's Committee on Full Employment and the
        Council of Social Planning of Alameda County.

601   _____, Ruth Schaffer, and Cecil Sheps.   1956.
        Community Organization: Action and Inaction.
        Chapel Hill: University of North Carolina Press.

602   Jennings, M. Kent. 1964. Community Influentials:
       The Elites of Atlanta. Glencoe, Ill.: The Free
       Press.
          Jennings found that not all of the central decision-
       makers came from the ranks of the economic domi-
       nants. Thus, he concludes that the notion of a high
       correlation between economic position and political
       power, even in the town studied by Floyd Hunter, is
       not always true. However, a coalition of power ac-
       tors, institutions, and organizations do tend to in-
       fluence the major decisions in Atlanta.

603   _____. 1961. "Political Statuses and Political
       Roles in Community Decision-Making." Unpublished
       Ph.D. dissertation, University of North Carolina.
          In 'Regional City,' Jennings found the power struc-
       ture to lie somewhere between monolithic and amor-
       phous. Attributed influentials did exercise power
       while economic dominants did not.

604   Jerovsek, Janez. 1966. "Socjalna Diferencijacija i
       Struktura Mori" [Social Differentiation and Power
       Structure]. Socijalizam 9: 378-382.
          It was found that social differentiation can hold
       back or impede the flow of power on the local level
       in Yugoslavia.

605   _____. 1970. "The Structure of Influence in the
       Yugoslav Commune." The New Atlantis 1 (Winter):
       31-47.

606   Joyner, Wilton Glenn. 1972. "A Study of the Commu-
       nity Power Structure in a Selected South Carolina
       County." Unpublished Ph.D. dissertation, University
       of South Carolina.
          Joyner found a high overlap (89%) between persons
       who were named as reputational leaders and those
       persons who were named as decisional leaders.
       There was no evidence that indicated a monolithic
       power structure so Joyner argued that there was a
       strong possibility of a pluralistic power structure.

607   Keil, Thomas J. 1971. "Community Specialization and
       Differentiation: A Study of Correlates of Policy Out-
       puts." Unpublished Ph.D. dissertation, Temple Uni-
       versity.

608   Kesl, Gary Lee. 1972. "Perceptions of the Community
       Power Structure of Selected Communities in South
       Florida." Unpublished Ph. D. dissertation, Univer-
       sity of Miami.
           A study of the power structure of the Homestead-
       Florida City area. Kesl found the power structure
       to be made up of a group of white, male individuals.
       He argues that the conservative nature of this group
       was a factor in the lack of community support for
       school policies.

609   Kesselman, Mark. 1967. The Ambiguous Consensus:
       A Study of Local Government in France. New York:
       Alfred A. Knopf.

610   Kimball, Solon T. and Marion Pearsall. 1954. The
       Talladega Story: A Study in Community Process.
       Birmingham: University of Alabama Press.

611   Kingsland, James Lyons. 1972. "Local Government
       Decision-Making in Sierra Leone." Unpublished
       Ph. D. dissertation, Northwestern University.

612   Klapp, Orrin and L. Vincent Padgett. 1960. "Power
       Structure and Decision-Making in a Mexican Border
       City." American Journal of   Sociology 45 (January):
       400-406.
           A study of the power structure of Tijiuana found
       that while there was a 'power elite' it was not very
       powerful.

613   Kolaczkowski, Andrzej. 1967. "Wyniki Pierwszejo
       Pilotazu Kwestionariusza do Badan nad Wladza
       Lokalna" [Results of a First Pilot Questionnaire of
       Research on Local Power]. Studia Socjologiczno
       Polityczne 23: 197-205.

614   Kornblum, William. 1970. "The Yugoslav Communal
       System: Decision-Making in Housing and Urban De-
       velopment." The New Atlantis 1 (Winter): 12-30.

615   Kuroda, Yasumasa. 1972. "Factions and Community
       Power Structure in Reed Town, Japan." Il Politico
       37 (June): 285-303.

616   _____. 1968. "Factions and Community Power
       Structure in Reed Town, Japan." Unpublished paper

presented at the meeting of the Association for Asian
Studies.

617 _____. 1967. "Psychological Aspects of Community
Power Structure: Leaders and Rank-and-File in
Reed Town, Japan." Southwestern Social Science
Quarterly 48 (December): 433-442.
Kuroda found that community leaders have a higher
sense of political obligation than the general population. Also, he found that the community leaders
were more pro-American and less authoritarian than
the general population.

618 _____. 1974. Reed Town in Japan: Community
Power Structure & Political Change. Honolulu:
University Press of Hawaii.

619 _____. 1973. Yoshikawa-Machi no Kenryoku Kozo
[Reed Town in Japan: Community Power Structure
& Political Change]. Tokyo: Keiso-Shobo.

620 Lamounier, B. 1968. "Politica Local e Tensões
Estruturais no Brasil: Teste Preliminar de uma
Hipostese" [Local Politics and Structural Stresses
in Brazil: Preliminary Testing of a Hypothesis].
Dados 4: 186-198.

621 Laquian, A. A. 1965. "Politics in Metropolitan
Manila." Philippine Journal of Public Administration 9 (October): 331-342.
Because of the large and diverse number of community groups, the political process in Manila was
found to be pluralistic.

622 Leif, Irving P. 1970. "The Application of Leadership
Networks to Community Power Structure." Unpub-
lished M.S. thesis, Purdue University.
A study of the secondary leaders in Lafayette,
Indiana.

623 _____. 1973 "The Structural Dimensions of Community Power: Toward a Redefinition and Codifica-
tion of the Concept of Community Power." Unpublished paper presented at the meeting of the Alpha
Kappa Delta Sociological Research Symposium.
A test of the Linton Freeman et al. theory of
community leadership. Using their technique of

resource network mapping, Leif found three levels of
leaders in his study of Lafayette, Indiana. Power
can be seen as the availability of resources within
and between organizations.

624 Lennarson, Ann L. 1967. "Power and Politics: Community Controversy." Unpublished M.S. thesis,
Northwestern University.

625 Levin, Murray B. 1960. The Alienated Voter: Politics
in Boston. New York: Holt, Rinehart and Winston, Inc.

626 Lindquist, John H. 1965. "An Occupational Analysis
of Local Politics: Syracuse, New York, 1880-1959."
Sociology and Social Research 49 (April): 343-354.

627 Lowry, Ritchie P. 1965. Who's Running This Town?
Community Leadership and Social Change. New
York: Harper & Row.
A study of community leadership and the relationship of the leadership group to social change. In the
small community, there was more opportunity for
potential mobilization for community action. This is
because community leaders are closer to the people
and the people are more active participants than in
larger communities.

628 _____. 1962. "Who Runs This Town? A Study of
the Quality of Public Life in a Changing Small Community." Unpublished Ph.D. dissertation, University
of California, Berkeley.

629 Lynd, Robert and Helen Lynd. 1929. Middletown.
New York: Harcourt, Brace and World.

630 _____, and _____. 1937. Middletown in Transition.
New York: Harcourt, Brace and World.

631 McClain, Jackson M., and Robert B. Highsaw. 1962.
Dixie City: A Study in Decision-Making. Birmingham:
Bureau of Public Admin., Univ. of Alabama.

632 McKee, James B. 1953. "Status and Power in the Industrial Community: A Comment on Drucker's Thesis."
American Journal of Sociology 58 (January): 364-70.

633 Marando, Vincent L. 1968. "Inter-Local Cooperation

in a Metropolitan Area: Detroit." <u>Urban Affairs</u>
<u>Quarterly</u> 4 (December):   185-201.

634   Marshall, Billie Jo.   1965.   "Social Power in Annville."
      Unpublished M.S. thesis, Iowa State University
      of Science and Technology.

635   Martin, Roscoe, Frank Munger, and others.   1961.
      <u>Decisions in Syracuse: A Metropolitan Action Study</u>.
      Bloomington: Indiana University Press.
         In a study of 22 decisions in Syracuse, the au-
      thors did not find evidence that a single-man mono-
      lithic power structure existed as had been reported
      earlier in studies of Syracuse.   They found as many
      decision centers as there were decision areas and
      that there were many ways of exercising community
      power.

636   Martindale, Don, and R. Gale Hanson.   1970.   <u>Small</u>
      <u>Town and the Nation: The Conflict of Local and</u>
      <u>Translocal Forces</u>.   Westport, Conn.:   Greenwood
      Pub. Corp.
         An examination of the conflicting forces of localism
      and cosmopolitanism.   The power structure in the
      community was divided between local and non-local
      interests.   The most noticeable conflict between these
      two interests was over the community's economy.

637   Meister, Albert.   1964.   "Diffusion et Concentration du
      Pouvoir dans une Commune Yougoslave" [Diffusion
      and Concentration of Power in a Yugoslavian Com-
      mune].   <u>Revue Française de Science Politique</u> 14
      (April):   268-293.
         In this Yugoslav commune, Meister found evidence
      to support the thesis of Djilas that power is concen-
      trated in the hands of those who hold ideological and
      formal power.   At the commune level, political ac-
      tivism does not confer monetary or material advan-
      tages.

638   Miller, D. F.   1965.   "Factions in Indian Village Poli-
      tics."   <u>Pacific Affairs</u> 38 (Spring):   17-31.

639   Miller, Delbert C.   1965.   "Community Power Perspec-
      tives and Role Definitions of North American Execu-
      tives in an Argentine Community."   <u>Administrative</u>
      <u>Science Quarterly</u> 10 (December):   364-380.

This study dispelled the notion that North American executives manipulated the power structure of the community. The executives were considered marginal members of the community.

640 _____. 1963. "Town and Gown: The Power Structure of a University Town." *American Journal of Sociology* 68 (January): 432-443.

Miller found that there was a cleavage between the town and the university. Because the community leaders were locals and the university leaders were cosmopolitans, the power flowed out of the community leaving it weaker.

641 _____, Eva Chamorro, and Juan Carlos Agulla. 1964. "La Estructura del Poder de una Ciudad Argentina" [The Structure of Power in an Argentina City]. *Cuadernos* 26 (October): 29-49.

642 _____, and James L. Dirksen. 1965. "The Identification of Visible, Concealed, and Symbolic Leaders in a Small Indiana City: A Replication of the Bonjean-Noland Study of Burlington, North Carolina." *Social Forces* 43 (May): 548-555.

A replication of the Bonjean-Noland study found similar data. Visible, concealed, and symbolic leaders were isolated in this Indiana community.

643 Miller, Michael V., and James D. Preston. 1973. "Vertical Ties and the Redistribution of Power in Crystal City." *Social Science Quarterly* 53 (March): 772-784.

Vertical ties contributed to the development of a pluralistic power structure in Crystal City. These extra-community resources helped lower socio-economic groups to participate more extensively in local community politics.

644 Mills, C. Wright, and Melville J. Ulmer. 1946. *Small Business and Civic Welfare.* Washington, D.C.: Report of the Small War Plants Corporation to the Special Committee to Study Problems of American Small Business. U.S. Senate, 79th Congress, 2nd Session, Document Number 135. Serial No. 11036.

645 Mills, Warner E., Jr., and Harry R. Davis. 1962.

Small City Government: Seven Cases in Decision
Making. New York: Random House.
Seven case studies of decision-making in Beloit,
Wisconsin, and the effects of these decisions on the
community.

646 Moore, Charles H. 1970. "The Politics of Urban
Violence: Policy Outcomes in Winston-Salem."
Social Science Quarterly 51 (September): 374-388.

647 _____. 1969. "The Politics of Urban Violence:
Policy Outcomes in Winston-Salem." Unpublished
paper presented at the meeting of the American
Political Science Association.

648 Mowitz, Robert J., and Deil S. Wright. 1962. Profile
of a Metropolis: A Case Book. Detroit: Wayne
State University Press.
Ten case studies of major community issues and
their outcomes in Detroit.

649 Muir, William K., Jr. 1958. Defending "The Hill"
Against Metal Houses. Birmingham: Inter-University
Case Program, University of Alabama.

650 Narojek, Winicjusz. 1967. "Struktura Wladzy Spolecznosci Lokalnej w Polsce" [The Structure of Local
Power in Poland]. Studia Socjologiczno Polityczne
23: 29-43.

651 O'Carroll, John Patrick. 1971. "Ecology and Perception of Community Power." Unpublished Ph.D. dissertation, Louisiana State University and Agricultural
and Mechanical College.
In this ecological analysis of community power
structure, O'Carroll found that perception levels
were related to social ties with the power structure.

652 _____, and Quentin A. L. Jenkins. 1971. "Ecology
and Perception of Community Power." Unpublished
paper presented at the meeting of the Rural Sociological Society.

653 Oldenburg, Philip K. 1967. "Indian Urban Politics
With Particular Reference to the Nagpur Corporation."
Unpublished M.A. thesis, University of Chicago.

654   Ostrowski, Krzysztof, and Adam Przeworski. 1967.
       "Decyzje Lokalnyck Systemow Politycznyck w Polsce"
       [Decisions of Local Political Systems in Poland].
       Studia Socjologiczno Polityczne 23: 83-93.

655   Pellegrin, Roland, and Charles Coates. 1956. "Ab-
       sentee-Owned Corporations and Community Power
       Structure." American Journal of Sociology 61
       (March): 413-419.
           It was found that the local corporations controlled
       the power in the community to the extent that their
       approval on an issue meant success for it and their
       disapproval on an issue meant failure for it.   Cor-
       poration executives participated in local community
       politics in accord with the needs of their corpora-
       tions.

656   Perrucci, Robert, and Marc Pilisuk. 1970. "Leaders
       and Ruling Elites: The Interorganizational Bases of
       Community Power." American Sociological Review
       35 (December): 1040-1057.
           In contrast with previous studies that viewed
       power through individuals, this study viewed power
       in terms of groups with interorganizational ties.
       These ties resulted in resource networks that could
       be used to mobilize power in order to influence the
       outcomes of community issues.

657   _____, and _____.   1969. "Leaders and Ruling
       Elites: The Interorganizational Bases of Community
       Power." Unpublished paper presented at the meet-
       ing of the American Sociological Association.

658   Pinard, Maurice. 1963. "Structural Attachments and
       Political Support in Urban Politics: The Case of
       Fluoridation Referendums." American Journal of
       Sociology 68 (March): 513-526.
           The degree of attachment between the community
       and its leaders greatly influences the support that it
       will give to those leaders. This support was in-
       fluenced by the size of the community, rate of growth,
       occupational and power structures, racial and ethnic
       makeup, and the state of the labor market.

659   Pouillon, Jean. 1964. "La Structure du Pouvoir Chez
       les Hadjerai (Tchad)" [The Structure of Power Among
       the Hadjerai]. L'Homme 4 (Sept.-Dec.): 18-70.

Pouillon found that political power was concentrated among the religious leaders in the community.

660 Presthus, Robert. 1964. Men at the Top: A Study of
     Community Power. New York: Oxford University
     Press.
     Presthus used two techniques (reputational and de-
     cisional) to locate power in two small communities.
     Both techniques yielded lists of leaders that were
     similar with a high amount of overlap. He concluded
     that both techniques should be used in future research.

661 Reichler, Melvin Litwack. 1963. "Community Power
     Structure in Action." Unpublished Ph. D. dissertation,
     University of Michigan.

662 Rhyne, Edwin H. 1957. "Party Politics and the De-
     cision Making Process: A Study at the County Level."
     Unpublished master's thesis, University of North
     Carolina.

663 Rogers, Robert Burtch. 1962. "Perception of the
     Power Structure by Social Class in a California Com-
     munity." Unpublished Ph. D. dissertation, University
     of Southern California.

664 Rossi, Peter H. 1956. "Historical Trends in the Poli-
     tics of an Industrial Community." Unpublished paper
     presented at the meeting of the American Sociological
     Society.

665 _____. 1961. "The Organizational Structure of an
     American Community." In Complex Organizations:
     A Sociological Reader, edited by Amitai Etzioni.
     New York: Holt, Rinehart & Winston. 301-312.

666 Salisbury, Robert H. 1960. "St. Louis Politics: Re-
     lationships Among Interests, Parties, and Govern-
     mental Structure." Western Political Quarterly 13
     (June): 498-507.

667 Sayre, Wallace S. , and Herbert Kaufman. 1965. Gov-
     erning New York City. New York: W. W. Norton.
     Sayre and Kaufman find a multiplicity of decision
     centers in New York City. The core of the decision
     group includes formal leaders, organized bureau-
     cracies, party leaders, and non-governmental

associations. None of these groups had enough power
to be self-sufficient. Major community decisions
were reached through bargaining and accommodation
between the participants.

668 Schaffer, Albert, and Ruth Connor Schaffer. 1970.
     Woodruff: A Study of Community Decision Making.
     Chapel Hill: University of North Carolina Press.
        It was found that the decision-makers of Woodruff
     were able to maintain their position without major
     opposition through three processes: non-decision-
     making, negative decision-making, and minimal sup-
     port for programs of change. The use of these
     methods has effectively maintained the power struc-
     ture throughout the postwar era.

669 Schmandt, Henry J. , Paul G. Steinbricker, and George
     P. Wendel. 1961. Metropolitan Reform in St. Louis.
     New York: Holt, Rinehart & Winston.

670 Schulze, Robert O. 1961. "The Bifurcation of Power
     in a Satellite City." In Community Political Systems,
     edited by Morris Janowitz. Glencoe, Ill. : The Free
     Press. 19-80.
        Schulze found that there had been a bifurcation of
     the economic and political dominants over a period of
     time in a midwestern city. Schulze was one of the
     first to stress the importance of absentee-ownership
     of industry. He found that absentee-ownership led to
     a withdrawl of economic dominants from community
     political affairs.

671 Scoble, Harry M. 1961. "Leadership Hierarchies and
     Political Issues in a New England Town." In Com-
     munity Political Systems, edited by Morris Janowitz.
     Glencoe, Ill. : The Free Press. 117-145.
        Leaders were found to be influential in specific
     areas or issues. There was no unitary power struc-
     ture in Bennington, Vermont. Power shifted from
     issue to issue.

672 _____. 1956. "Yankeetown: Leadership in Three
     Decision-Making Processes." Unpublished paper pre-
     sented at the meeting of the American Political
     Science Association.

673 _____. 1957. "Yankeetown: A Study of Community

Decision-Making Processes." Unpublished Ph.D.
dissertation, Yale University.

674   Scott, Stanley, and John C. Bollens. 1968. Governing
a Metropolitan Region: The San Francisco Bay Area.
Berkeley: Institute for Governmental Studies, University of California, Berkeley.

675   Seasholes, Bradbury. 1962. "Patterns of Influence in
Metropolitan Boston." In Current Trends in Com-
parative Community Studies, edited by Bert Swanson.
Kansas City, Mo.: Community Studies. 60-68.

676   Smallwood, Frank. 1965. Greater London: The Politics of Metropolitan Reform. Indianapolis: Bobbs-
Merrill.

677   Smith, Lincoln. 1963. "Power Politics in Brunswick:
A Case Study." Human Organization 22 (Summer):
152-158.
        A case study of Brunswick, Maine. Smith argues
that reform movements toward nonpartisanship in local politics may cause a loss of interest in local
government by community residents.

678   Smith, P. A. 1965. "The Games of Community Politics." Midwest Journal of Political Science 9
(February): 37-60.

679   Smith, Ted C. 1958. "Power and Influences in a
Changing Suburban Community." Unpublished Ph.D.
dissertation, University of Utah.

680   _____. 1960. "The Structure of Power in a Suburban Community." Pacific Sociological Review 3
(Fall): 83-88.
        There was a general structuring of power in the
community into a single hierarchy based on residence
commitment rather than on economic dominance.

681   Sofen, Edward. 1963. The Miami Metropolitan Experiment. Bloomington: Indiana University Press.
        During its first five years of existence, Metro
Miami had suffered from inadequate local leadership.

682   Springfield Area Movement for a Democratic Society.
1971. "Power Elite in Springfield, Massachusetts."

Unpublished paper presented at the meeting of the
American Sociological Association.

683 Starr, Roger. 1969. "The Mayor's Dilemmas--I:
Power and Powerlessness in a Regional City." The
Public Interest 16 (Summer): 3-24.

684 Stewart, Frank. 1947. "A Sociometric Study of Influence in Southtown." Sociometry 10 (February):
11-31.

685 _____. 1947. "A Study of Influence in Southtown, II."
Sociometry 10 (August): 273-286.

686 Stewart, Philip D. 1968. Political Power in the
Soviet Union: A Study of Decision-Making in Stalin-
grad. Indianapolis: Bobbs-Merrill.

687 Stinchcombe, Jean L. 1968. Reform and Reaction:
City Politics in Toledo. Belmont, Cal.: Wadsworth
Pub. Co.

688 Stone, Clarence N. 1963. "The City Manager and
Community Power: Leadership and Policy Making
in a Council-Manager City." Unpublished Ph.D.
dissertation, Duke University.

689 Swanson, Bert E. 1959. "Power and Politics: A
Community Formulates Electric Power Policy."
Unpublished Ph.D. dissertation, University of
Oregon.
      Swanson found that participants in the community
controversy over electric power manipulated the conflict for personal career objectives. They also tried
to reduce the intensity of the conflict so that other
community actors would not become involved.

690 Tarkowski, Jacek. 1967. "Study of the Decision Process in Rolnowo Poviat." Polish Sociological Bulletin 16: 89-96.

691 Teague, Richard L. 1969. "Community Power and
Social Change: A Case for Social Action." Unpublished Ph.D. dissertation, North Carolina State University, Raleigh.
      A study of the transition of a community from a
rural economic base to an industrialized economic

base and how the power structure reacted to these
structural changes.

692 Thernstrom, Stephen. 1965. " 'Yankee City' Revisited:
The Perils of Historical Naivete." American Sociological Review 30 (April): 234-242.
A critique of Warner's Yankee City study based
on careful reconstruction of events from original
nineteenth-century sources.

693 Thometz, Carol E. 1963. The Decision-Makers: The
Power Structure of Dallas. Dallas: Southern Metho-
dist University Press.
Thometz found that a concentrated group of men
and associations exercised the major influence on a
number of community decisions. These decision-
makers stressed no party affiliations and were very
loyal to Dallas. The decision-makers worked in the
open, and despite opposition, there was no evidence
that they did not work for the good of Dallas.

694 Van Den Berghe, Pierre L. 1964. Caneville: The
Social Structure of a South African Town. Middletown, Conn.: Wesleyan University Press.
Van den Berghe found the power structure of
Caneville to be 'paternalistic'. The distribution of
power was related to the economic position of community actors.

695 Vanderbok, William G. 1969. "Decisions and Nondecisions: Elite Structures and Political Power in an
Indian City." Unpublished Ph.D. dissertation, Indiana University.

696 Vetterli, R. Richard. 1972. "The Impact of the
Multinational Corporation on the Power Structure
of Mexico and a Mexican Border Community." Unpublished Ph.D. dissertation, University of California, Riverside.

697 Vidich, Arthur J., and Joseph Bensman. 1958. Small
Town in Mass Society. Princeton, N.J.: Princeton
University Press.

698 Walter, Benjamin. 1960. "Communications and Influence: Decision-Making in a Municipal Administrative Hierarchy." Unpublished Ph.D. dissertation,
Northwestern University.

699   _____. 1962. "Political Decision-Making in Arcadia."
       In Urban Group Dynamics, edited by F. Stuart Chapin,
       Jr. and Shirley F. Weiss. New York: John Wiley
       & Sons. 141-186.
           A case study of three community issues and their
       outcomes in the community of Arcadia. The eco-
       nomic elite in Arcadia did not control the decision-
       making process.

700   Warner, W. Lloyd, and associates. 1949. Democracy
       in Jonesville. New York: Harper and Brothers.

701   _____, J. O. Low, Paul S. Hunt, and Leo Srole.
       1963. Yankee City. New Haven, Conn.: Yale Uni-
       versity Press (abridged edition).

702   Warren, Elizabeth A. C. 1970. "The Anatomy of De-
       cision Making in a Local Community: A Study of
       Kansas City." Unpublished Ph. D. dissertation, Uni-
       versity of Nebraska.

703   Weiner, Myron. 1961. "Violence and Politics in Calcutta."
       Journal of Asian Politics 20 (February): 275-281.

704   Wellman, Frederick L. 1963. "Interrelationships and
       Operational Patterns of Leaders in the Power Struc-
       ture of a Selected County." Unpublished Ed. D. dis-
       sertation, University of Florida.

705   Westland, Charles. 1971. "Citizen Preferences and
       Governmental Decisions." Unpublished paper pre-
       sented at the meeting of the Society for the Study
       of Social Problems.

706   Wiebe, Paul. 1969. "Elections in Peddui: Democracy
       at Work in an Indian Town." Human Organization 28
       (Summer): 140-147.
           A study of the role that the power structure
       played in the electoral process in Peddui. It was
       found that traditional Indian social structure continues
       to have the most powerful influence on the democratic
       process.

707   Wildavsky, Aaron. 1964. Leadership in a Small Town.
       Totowa, New Jersey: Bedminster Press.
           Wildavsky, using the decision-making approach,
       replicated Dahl's study of New Haven in Oberlin,

Ohio. He found similar results in Oberlin: a pluralist power structure where the decisive influence
on community decisions shifts with issue area. The
study also provides a valuable portrayal of a dynamic
city manager, a careful interpretation of budget prep-
aration, and a survey of knowledge of community decisions by the general public.

708 Williams, Oliver P., Harold Herman, Charles S.
Lieberman, and Thomas R. Dye. 1965. Suburban
Differences and Metropolitan Policies: A Philadelphia Story. Philadelphia: The University of Penn-
sylvania Press.

709 Wirt, Frederick M. 1970. "Alioto and the Politics of
Hyperpluralism." Transaction 7 (April): 46-55.

710 Wood, Thomas J. 1964. "Dade County: Unbossed,
Erratically Led." The Annals of the American
Academy of Political and Social Science 353 (May):
64-71.
Political leadership in Dade County was usually of
short duration. The newspapers wielded an unusual
amount of influence in the area because of the de-
pendence of newcomers on them.

711 Zelliot, Eleanor. 1966. "Buddhism and Politics in
Maharashtra." In South Asian Politics and Religion,
edited by Donald E. Smith. Princeton, N.J.:
Princeton University Press. 191-212.

STUDIES OF COMMUNITY LEADERSHIP

712 Abu-Laban, Baha. 1961. "Leadership Visibility in a
Local Community." Pacific Sociological Review 4
(Fall): 73-78.
Leader visibility was determined by the perceiver
and the object of perception as well as the interactive
effect on each other. Other factors such as social
participation, social class, sex, length of community
residence, and involvement in community affairs were
also important in determining the public's awareness
of them.

713 _____. 1963. "Self-Conception and Appraisal by

Others: A Study of Community Leaders." Sociology
and Social Research 48 (October): 32-37.

714 _____. 1963. "Social Origins and Occupational
Career Patterns of Community Leaders." Sociological Inquiry 33 (Spring): 131-140.
    This study revealed similar findings to other
studies of leader characteristics. The social origins
of community leaders were generally non-manually
oriented occupations, high levels of education, long
community residence, active participation in voluntary
associations, and were generally older men.

715 _____. 1960. "Visibility of Community Leaders."
Unpublished Ph.D. dissertation, University of
Washington.

716 Acker, Roy Dean. 1963. "The Influentials in a Selected County and Their Involvement in the Decision-
Making Process." Unpublished Ed.D. dissertation,
University of Florida.
    This study identified key influentials in a county
and their relationship to the decision-making process.
Implications for education in relation to the power
structure were also discussed.

717 Adrian, Charles. 1966. Community Leadership and
Decision-Making. Iowa City: Institute of Public
Affairs, University of Iowa.

718 _____. 1959. "The Role of the City Council in
Community Policy-Making." Unpublished paper pre-
sented at the meeting of the American Political
Science Association.

719 Akimoto, Ritsuo. 1966. "Community Power Structure
and Leadership Formation." Shakaigaku Hyoron 16
(June): 2-19.

720 Babchuk, Nicholas, Ruth Marsey, and C. Wayne Gordon.
1960. "Men and Women in Community Agencies: A
Note on Power and Prestige." American Sociological
Review 25 (June): 399-403.
    This was a study of the role of women in the
power structure of a community. It was found that
women were more likely to be found as influentials
in small voluntary organizations and agencies rather
than the larger ones.

721   Banfield, Edward C. , and James Q. Wilson. 1967.
      "Power Structure and Civic Leadership. " In Metrop-
      olis in Crisis, edited by Jeffrey K. Hadden, Louis
      Massotti, and Calvin J. Larson. Itasca, Ill. :
      F. E. Peacock. 417-432.

722   Berger, S. , P. Gourevitch, P. Higonnet, and K. Kaiser.
      1969. "The Problem of Reform in France: The
      Political Ideas of Local Elites. " Political Science
      Quarterly 84 (September): 436-460.

723   Bohlen, Joe M. , George M. Beal, Gerald E. Klonglan,
      and John L. Tait. 1965. Community Power Actors
      and Civil Defense. Ames: Rural Sociology Report
      No. 40, Department of Economics and Sociology,
      Iowa State University of Science and Technology.

724   Bonjean, Charles M. 1963. "Community Leadership:
      A Case Study and Conceptual Refinement. " American
      Journal of Sociology 68 (May): 672-681.
         Arguments against the use of the reputational
      technique for identifying community leaders are an-
      swered in this study.   Bonjean refines the technique
      and uses sociometric techniques to supplement his
      results.   He found three types of community leaders:
      visible leaders who play the roles that the community
      perceives them of playing, concealed leaders who
      play a larger role in the power structure than the
      community realized, and symbolic leaders who did
      not yield as much power as the community perceived.
      The 'Bonjean technique' for identifying these three
      types of reputational leaders has been used in many
      subsequent studies.

725   _____. 1963. "Community Leadership: A Concep-
      tual Refinement and Comparative Analysis. " Un-
      published Ph. D. dissertation, University of North
      Carolina.

726   Bradley, Donald S. 1971. "Community Leadership in
      the Inner-City. " Unpublished paper presented at the
      meeting of the Southern Sociological Society.

727   _____, and Mayer N. Zald. 1965. "From Commer-
      cial Elite to Political Administrator: The Recruit-
      ment of the Mayors of Chicago. " American Journal
      of Sociology 71 (September): 153-167.

Chicago's early mayors were drawn from its com-
mercial leaders regardless of family background.
There was a period of transitional mayors which
then was followed by a group of mayors who were
social notables or businessmen highly involved in
politics.   Finally, the Democratic political machine
began to dominate and continues to do so at present.

728   Brierly, T. G.   1966.   "The Evolution of Local Administration in French-Speaking West Africa."   Journal
of Local Administration Overseas 5 (January):   56-
71.

729   Brown, Anna B.   1964.   "Women Influentials."   Journal
of Cooperative Extension 2 (Summer):   97-104.

730   Buck, Robert E.   1970.   "Power, Ideology, and Decision-Making: An Investigation in the Social Psychology of Community Politics."   Unpublished Ph. D.
dissertation, University of Texas.
A study of the social psychological attitudes of
leaders in five communities.   From this data, the
place of individual leaders in the decision-making
process was examined.

731   Church, Roderick.   1973.   "Authority and Influence in
Indian Municipal Politics: Administrators and
Councillors in Sucknow."   Asian Survey 13 (April):
421-438.

732   Clark, Peter.   1960.   "Civic Leadership: The Symbols
of Legitimacy."   Unpublished paper presented at the
meeting of the American Political Science Association.

733   Dahl, Robert.   1959.   "Patrician and Plebian."   Unpublished paper presented at the meeting of the
American Sociological Association.

734   Dahlberg, Frances.   1971.   "Centralization and Change
in the Governing Elite: Lira, Uganda."   Unpublished
paper presented at the meeting of the American Sociological Association.

735   Daland, Robert T.   1956.   Dixie City: A Portrait of
Political Leadership.   Birmingham: University of
Alabama, Bureau of Public Administration.

736 D'Antonio, William V. 1966. "Community Leadership
     in an Economic Crisis: Testing Ground for Ideolog-
     ical Cleavage." American Journal of Sociology 71
     (May): 688-700.

737 Fanelli, A. Alexander. 1956. "A Typology of Com-
     munity Leadership Based on Influence and Interaction
     Within the Leadership Subsystem." Social Forces
     34 (May): 332-338.
          In this study of a small Mississippi community,
     the relationships among leaders and the subsequent
     leadership subsystem was examined. It was found
     that leadership was specialized with the leadership
     subsystem supporting the specialized leader.

738 Form, William H. , and Warren L. Sauer. 1960.
     Community Influentials in a Middle-Sized City: A
     Case Study. East Lansing: Michigan State Univer-
     sity.
          This study isolated community influentials in East
     Lansing, Michigan, and compared them to the Для-
     tune '900'. The influentials were found to be very
     similar to the '900' in education, social background,
     age, length of residence in the community, organi-
     zational tenure, and employment mobility. The in-
     fluentials themselves, were composed primarily of
     businessmen who perceived their roles as that of
     community activists and decision-makers.

739 Frolic, B. Michael. 1970. "Soviet Urban Political
     Leaders." Comparative Political Studies 2 (January):
     443-464.

740 Gabias, S. T. 1964. "Leadership in a Large Manager
     City: The Case of Kansas City." The Annals of the
     American Academy of Political and Social Science
     353 (May): 52-63.
          An examination of the city manager in Kansas
     City and his relationships with other government
     officials. Gabias argues that improvements are
     necessary in the leadership structure above the
     city manager.

741 Galbo, Charles Joseph. 1962. "Personality and In-
     fluence in a Community Power Structure." Unpub-
     lished Ph. D. dissertation, University of Arizona.
          A study of the personality patterns of the power

elite in a southwestern American community. Using
the 16 Personality Factor Questionnaire, Galbo found
a number of personality factors to be significant
among all the members of the power elite.

742 Gallo, Vincent A. 1968. "A Comparative Study of Occupational Prestige and Social Associations Among
Community Leaders." Unpublished Ph. D. dissertation, University of Oregon.

743 Grant, W. P. 1970. "Rancorous Community Conflict:
A Study of Political Leaders in Two Scottish New
Towns." International Review of Community Develop-
ment 23-24 (December): 199-218.

744 Hacker, A. , and Aberbach, J. D. 1962. "Businessmen in Politics." Law and Contemporary Problems
27 (Spring): 266-279.

745 Hicks, Frederic. 1967. "Politics, Power, and the
Role of the Village Priest in Paraguay." Journal
of Inter-American Studies 9 (April): 273-282.

746 Holderman, James Bowker. 1962. "Decision Making
and Community Leadership in the Village of Winnetka,
Illinois." Unpublished Ph. D. dissertation, Northwestern University.

747 Jenkins, Quentin A. L. 1966. "Community Actor's
Perceptions of Community Power Structure." Unpublished Ph. D. dissertation, University of Iowa.

748 Jones, Herbert Kelly, Jr. 1970. "Community Leadership and Economic Growth." Unpublished Ph. D.
dissertation, North Texas State University.

749 Jones, Joseph H. , Jr. 1956. "A Comparative Analy-
sis of Community Leaders and Non-Leaders in a
North Central Kentucky Community." Unpublished
Ph. D. dissertation, University of Kentucky.

750 Kammerer, Gladys M. , and J. M. DeGrove. 1964.
"Urban Leadership During Change." The Annals of
the American Academy of Political and Social Science
353 (May): 95-106.
        Kammerer and DeGrove examine different styles
of political leadership and conclude that a competitive

style of politics will produce the community's most
effective source of leadership.

751 Kaufman, Harold F., and Kenneth P. Wilkinson. 1967.
     Community Structure and Leadership: An Interactive
     Perspective in the Study of Community. State Col-
     lege: Mississippi State University Social Science
     Research Center Bulletin 13.

752 Kavanagh, D. 1967. "The Orientations of Community
     Leaders to Parliamentary Candidates." Political
     Studies 15 (October): 351-356.

753 Kelner, Merrijoy. 1970. "Ethnic Penetration into
     Toronto's Elite Structure." Canadian Review of
     Sociology & Anthropology 7 (May): 128-137.
          The elite concept was broadened to include pres-
     tige as well as power and functional importance.
     The ethnic composition of the upper core elite as
     well as the lower functional elite was examined and
     non-Anglo-Saxon penetration was assessed.

754 Kimbrough, Emory, Jr. 1958. "The Role of the
     Banker in a Small City." Social Forces 36 (May):
     316-322.
          It was found that power on the community level
     was equated with economic interests. In this study,
     the bankers used the capital in their banks to in-
     crease their own power.

755 Kimbrough, Ralph. 1953. "The Operational Beliefs of
     Selected Leaders in a Selected County." Unpublished
     Ed. D. dissertation, University of Tennessee.

756 Kingdon, J. W. 1970. "Opinion Leaders in the Elec-
     torate." Public Opinion Quarterly 34 (Summer):
     256-261.

757 Kjellberg, Franceso. 1965. "Politisk Lederskap i en
     Utkantkommune" [Political Leadership in a Suburban
     Community]. Tidsskrift for Samfunnsforskning 6:
     74-90.

758 Klein, Henry Louis. 1965. "Community Organization
     Leadership in Philadelphia." Unpublished Ed. D.
     dissertation, Temple University.

759 Kolaja, Jiri. 1971. "Images of the Future by Commu-
    nity Leaders and by Workers." Unpublished paper
    presented at the meeting of the American Sociologi-
    cal Association.

760 Kuroda, Yasumasa. 1965-66. "Political Role Attribu-
    tions and Dynamics in a Japanese Community."
    Public Opinion Quarterly 29 (Winter): 602-613.

761 Lakshminarayana, H. D. 1969. "Leadership and
    Political Development in a Mysore Village: A Case
    Study." Journal of Social Research 12 (March): 17-
    26.

762 Larson, Calvin J. 1967. "The Economic History of a
    Community and the Character of Its Leadership: A
    Comparative Analysis." Unpublished paper presented
    at the meeting of the Ohio Valley Sociological Society.

763 _____, and Harry R. Potter. 1971. "Leadership,
    Socioeconomic Status, and Awareness of Poverty."
    Social Science Quarterly 52 (September): 261-276.

764 _____, and _____. 1970. "Leadership, Socio-
    economic Status, and Awareness of Poverty." Un-
    published paper presented at the meeting of the
    American Sociological Association.

765 Lindquist, John Henry. 1961. "Businessmen in Poli-
    tics: An Analysis of Political Participation in Syra-
    cuse, N. Y., 1880-1959." Unpublished Ph. D. disser-
    tation, Syracuse University.

766 _____. 1964. "Socioeconomic Status and Political
    Participation." Western Political Quarterly 17
    (December): 608-614.

767 Locke, Katherine, Edwin A. Locke, and Lois R. Dean.
    1966. "A Comparison of the Attitudes of Civil De-
    fense Directors and Community Leaders." Journal
    of Applied Behavioral Science 2 (Oct.-Dec.): 413-
    430.
        Locke, Locke, and Dean found that the relative
    lack of success of civil defense in this country was
    partly the result of differences in attitudes between
    local community leaders (who can grant civil defense
    funds) and local civil defense directors (who request
    the funds).

768 Lowe, Francis E., and Thomas C. McCormick. 1956-
       57. "A Study of the Influence of Formal and Infor-
       mal Leaders in an Election Campaign." Public
       Opinion Quarterly 20 (Winter): 651-662.
         The political opinions of community residents were
       relatively independent of those opinions attributed to
       their leaders.

769 Lowry, Ritchie P. 1964. "Leadership Interaction in
       Group Consciousness and Social Change." Pacific
       Sociological Review 7 (Spring): 22-29.

770 _____. 1965. "Mediating Leadership and Community
       Interaction." In Applied Sociology: Opportunities and
       Problems, edited by Alvin Gouldner and S. M. Miller.
       New York: The Free Press. 226-236.
         Lowry proposed the concept of the mediating leader
       who was a member of both local and cosmopolitan in-
       fluential groups. The mediating leader was best
       equipped to facilitate leadership interaction and mo-
       bilize these groups for community decision-making.
       If the mediating leader does not facilitate this inter-
       action, the confrontation of local and cosmopolitan
       interests could be disruptive to the community.

771 Luttbeg, Norman R. 1969. "The Representative Quality
       of Community Leaders' Policy Preferences." Re-
       search Reports in Social Science 12 (August): 17-31.

772 _____. 1968. "The Structure of Beliefs Among
       Leaders and the Public." Public Opinion Quarterly
       32 (Fall): 398-409.
         In contrast to earlier studies, Luttbeg found the
       belief systems of leaders to be multidimensional as
       well as unidimensional in nature.

773 Matthews, Thomas. 1953. "The Lawyer as Community
       Leader: One Dimension of the Professional Role."
       Unpublished Ph.D. dissertation, Cornell University.

774 Meredith, William V. 1963. "Comparisons of Liberal-
       Conservative Socio-Economic Value Measurements Be-
       tween Influentials and Persons Residing in Two Se-
       lected Florida Counties." Unpublished Ph.D. disser-
       tation, University of Florida.

775 Miller, Delbert C. 1956. "The Seattle Business

Leader." <u>Pacific Northwest Business</u> 15 (February): 5-12.

776 Monsen, J., and M. Cannon. 1965. <u>The Makers of Public Policy: American Power Groups and Their Ideologies</u>. New York: McGraw-Hill.

777 Moriarty, Thomas E. 1956. "A Study of Leadership Behavior in the Youth Serving Agencies of an Oregon Community." Unpublished Ph. D. dissertation, University of Oregon.

778 Morris, D. S., and K. Newton. 1970. "Profile of a Local Political Elite: Businessmen as Community Decision-Makers in Birmingham, 1838-1966." <u>The New Atlantis</u> 1 (Winter): 111-123.

779 Mulford, Charles L. 1967. "Considerations of the Instrumental and Expressive Roles of Community Influentials and Formal Organizations." <u>Sociology and Social Research</u> 51 (January): 141-147.
      Community roles among influential leaders were found to be consensual in character. Mulford found that higher status formal organizations were instrumental and expressive rather than instrumental or expressive.

780 _____. 1966. "On Role Consensus About Community Leaders." <u>Sociological Inquiry</u> 36 (Winter): 15-18.
      In samples of two communities (rural and non-rural) and a group of 'influentials' in the nonrural community, there was a high consensus among the three samples on the role a community leader was expected to play.

781 Nett, Emily M. 1971. "The Functional Elites of Quito." <u>Journal of Inter-American Studies and World Affairs</u> 13 (January): 112-120.

782 Nix, Harold L. 1970. <u>Identification of Leaders, and Their Involvement in the Planning Process</u>. Washington, D. C.: Public Health Service Publication No. 1998, U. S. Department of Health, Education, and Welfare.

783 _____, and Ram N. Singh. 1970. "Differential Views of Leader Respondents and Random Respondents

in a Community Social Analysis." Unpublished paper
presented at the meeting of the Rural Sociological
Society.

784 Olmstead, Donald W. 1954. "Organizational Leadership and Social Structure in a Small City." American Sociological Review 19 (June): 273-281.

785 Patnaik, N. 1969. "Profile of Leadership in Ruriban,
a Peasant Community in Orissa." Behavioral
Sciences and Community Development 3 (September):
83-100.

786 Plunkett, H. Dudley, and Mary Jean Bowman. 1973.
Elites and Change in the Kentucky Mountains. Lex-
ington: The University Press of Kentucky.

787 Powers, Ronald C. 1966. "The Incidence of Women in
Community Power Structures." Unpublished paper
presented at the meeting of the Rural Sociological
Society.

788 Present, Phillip Edward. 1967. "Defense Contracting
and Community Leadership: A Comparative Analysis."
Southwestern Social Science Quarterly 48 (December):
399-410.
    Defense contracting caused changes in the leader-
ship structure in two communities. With the development of large, modern, defense-oriented industries,
the engineers and managers working in them grad-
ually displaced the traditional community leaders.

789 Rosenthal, Donald B., and Robert L. Crain. 1966.
"Executive Leadership and Community Innovation:
The Fluoridation Experience." Urban Affairs Quarterly 1 (March): 39-57.
    Rosenthal and Crain found that American mayors
and managers have supported fluoridation very fre-
quently even when it was politically unwise. The
positions of these local political leaders were crucial
in many instances in the outcome of the fluoridation
issue. In addition, these leaders can influence the
outcome of the fluoridation issue in their communities
by providing 'cues' to the public on the issue.

790 Ruchelman, Leonard J., editor. 1969. Big City
Mayors. Bloomington: Indiana University Press.

791 Schulze, Robert O. 1956. "Economic Dominants and
     Public Leadership." Unpublished Ph. D. dissertation,
     University of Michigan.

792 _____. 1958. "The Role of Economic Dominants in
     Community Power Structure." American Sociological
     Review 23 (February): 3-9.
         A historical study of economic dominants in
     'Cibola' revealed that as corporations have increased
     in size and scope, the economic dominants have in-
     creasingly withdrawn from local political affairs.
     Schulze found that a bifurcation had taken place be-
     tween the economic and political spheres.

793 Shamir, S. 1961. "Temurot Be-Hanehaga Ha-Kfarit
     Shel Ar-Ramon" [Changes in the Village Leadership
     at Ar-Rama]. Hamizrah Hehadash 11: 241-257.

794 Shoemaker, Donald J., and Harold L. Nix. 1972.
     "A Study of Reputational Community Leaders Using
     the Concepts of Exchange and Coordinative Positions."
     The Sociological Quarterly 13 (Fall): 516-524.

795 _____, and _____. 1969. "A Study of Reputa-
     tional Community Leaders Using the Concepts of Ex-
     change and Coordinative Positions." Unpublished
     paper presented at the meeting of the Southern Socio-
     logical Society.

796 Shrader, Lawrence, and Ram Joshi. 1963. "Zilla
     Parishad Elections in Maharashtra and the District
     Political Elite." Asian Survey 3 (March): 143-155.

797 Siegel, Robert S., and H. Paul Friesema. 1965. "Ur-
     ban Community Leaders' Knowledge of Public Opinion."
     Western Political Quarterly 18 (December): 891-895.

798 Smith, Lincoln. 1955. "Political Leadership in a New
     England Community." Review of Politics 17 (July):
     392-409.

799 Smuckler, Ralph, and George M. Belknap. 1956.
     Leadership and Participation in Urban Political Af-
     fairs. East Lansing: Government Research Bureau,
     Michigan State University.

800 Sofen, Edward. 1961. "Problems of Metropolitan

Leadership: The Miami Experience." Midwest
Journal of Political Science 5 (February): 18-38.

801   Speight, John F.   1968.   "Community Homogeneity and
Consensus on Leadership." Sociological Quarterly
9 (Summer): 387-396.

802   _____.   1965.   "Community Homogeneity and Consensus on Leadership." Unpublished master's thesis, North Carolina State University.

803   Storer, N. W.   1956.   "Patterns of Change in the
Leadership of a Small Community." Unpublished
master's thesis, University of Kansas.

804   Sutton, Willis A. , Jr.   1972.   "Visible, Symbolic, and
Concealed Leaders in a Kentucky County: A Repli-
cation and Comparisons With Other Communities."
The Sociological Quarterly 13 (Summer): 409-418.

805   Tait, John L. , and Joe M. Bohlen.   1967.   "The Ex-
pected Role Performance of Community Power Actors
in Five Iowa Communities." Unpublished paper presented at the meeting of the Rural Sociological Society.

806   Van der Merwe, Hendrick Willem.   1963.   "Leadership
in a Saskatchewan Community: The Impact of Industrialization." Unpublished Ph. D. dissertation, University of California, Los Angeles.

807   Watson, James B. , and Julian Samora.   1954.   "Subordinate Leadership in a Bi-Cultural Community:
An Analysis." American Sociological Review 19
(August): 413-421.
A study of the relationship of the subordinate
leaders in a Spanish sub-community and the Anglo
leadership structure of that community.

808   Wells, Lloyd M.   1967.   "Social Values and Political
Orientations of City Managers: A Survey Report."
Southwestern Social Science Quarterly 48 (December):
443-450.
This study of the reading habits, life style, and
value patterns of city managers suggests that they
are broadly similar, although slightly more liberal
than business executives of similar education and
income.

809 Williams, Anne, and William Lassey. 1970. "Leader-
     ship and Community Development in a Bi-Cultural
     Setting." Unpublished paper presented at the meet-
     ing of the Rural Sociological Society.

810 Willie, Charles, Herbert Notkin, and Nicholas Rezak.
     1964. "Trends in the Participation of Businessmen
     in Local Community Voluntary Affairs." Sociology
     and Social Research 48 (April): 389-400.
         A study of the leadership structure of Syracuse,
     New York. It was found that economic dominants
     were not withdrawing from community affairs as had
     been reported in other studies. Businessmen were
     expanding their participation in local affairs also.

811 Zald, Mayer N., and T. A. Anderson. 1968. "Secular
     Trends and Historical Contingencies in the Recruit-
     ment of Mayors: Nashville as Compared to New
     Haven and Chicago." Urban Affairs Quarterly 4
     (June): 53-68.

STUDIES AROUND SPECIFIC COMMUNITY ISSUES

Education

812 Agger, Robert E. 1960. "The Politics of Local Edu-
     cation: A Comparative Study of Community Decision-
     Making." In A Forward Look: The Preparation of
     School Administrators, 1970, edited by Donald E.
     Tope. Eugene: Bureau of Education Research, Uni-
     versity of Oregon. 131-157.

813 Beal, George M., John J. Hartman, and Virginia
     Lagomareino. 1968. "An Analysis of Factors As-
     sociated With School Bond Elections." Rural So-
     ciology 33 (September): 313-327.
         Little relationship was found between election out-
     come and the techniques that educators felt were im-
     portant to insure the passage of school bond issues.

814 Blome, Arvin Chris. 1963. "A Study in the Identifica-
     tion of Community Power Structure and Influence on
     Public School Issues." Unpublished Ph.D. disserta-
     tion, State University of Iowa.
         An examination of the problems of school reorgan-
     ization and school bond issues and the relationship

of these issues to the community power structure.

815 Bloomberg, Warner, Jr. , and Morris Sunshine. 1963.
     Suburban Power Structures and Public Education.
     Syracuse, N.Y. : Syracuse University Press.

816 Braun, Harry Jean, III. 1971. "The Evaluation of
     Power as It Is Related to the Involvement of Lay
     Leadership in School Community Relations. " Un-
     published Ed. D. dissertation, University of Missouri,
     Columbia.

817 Brown, Anna B. 1963. "A Study of Women Influentials
     in Three Michigan Communities: Their Attitudes
     Towards and Perceived Ability to Influence Adult
     Education Practices. " Unpublished Ph. D. disserta-
     tion, University of Michigan.
         A sociometric study was conducted to isolate those
     women reputed to have influence in community affairs.
     Personal interviews were conducted with these women
     to determine their attitudes toward adult education.
     The women believed that they could influence educa-
     tional practices.

818 Crain, Robert L. , and associates. 1968. The Politics
     of School Desegregation: Comparative Case Studies
     of Community Structure and Policy Making. Chicago:
     Aldine Pub. Co.
         Crain and his associates visited cities in both the
     North and South of the U. S. in an effort to uncover
     different patterns of decision-making relating to
     school desegregation (primarily defined as increasing
     the mixture of white and black pupils within each
     school). In more decentralized cities, with weak
     political leaders, civic elite groups were especially
     important in influencing the school board and desegre-
     gation decisions. In more centralized cities, where
     the mayor often appointed the school board or in-
     fluenced school board decisions, decisions were gen-
     erally made with less controversy. And it was in
     more centralized cities that desegregation tended to
     be achieved more rapidly and effectively.

819 _____, and David Street. 1966. "School Desegrega-
     tion and School Decision-Making. " Urban Affairs
     Quarterly 2 (September): 64-82.
         The bureaucracy of public schools and the process

of decision-making within the school system was examined.   It was found that while the bureaucratic
leadership had very little direct power, the school
board and other civic elites could influence decisions
by setting a political style that was adopted by other
people in the decision-making process.

820   Cramer, M. Richard.   1963.   "School Desegregation
and New Industry: The Southern Community Leaders'
Viewpoint."   Social Forces 41 (May):   384-389.
      After a study of the leaders in five southern com-
munities, Cramer concluded that the impetus for
equal rights for Negroes will have to come from
someplace other than the recognized white community leadership.

821   Cunningham, Luvern L.   1964.   "Community Power:
Implications for Education."   In The Politics of Education in the Local Community, edited by Robert S.
Cahill and Stephen Hencley.   Danville, Ill.:   Interstate Printers & Publishers.   27-50.

822   Eliot, Thomas H.   1959.   "Toward an Understanding of
Public School Politics."   American Political Science
Review 53 (December):   1032-1051.
      Eliot argues that a continuing analysis of public
school politics is necessary in order to document the
aims and achievements of local communities in education.   Since local school systems are run by local
politicians, an understanding of power groups will be
necessary in order to understand public school policies.

823   Gittell, Marilyn.   1970.   "Urban School Politics: Pro-
fessionalism vs. Reform."   Journal of Social Issues
26 (Summer):   69-84.
      A discussion of the decentralization-community con-
trol school system and the political battle between
school professionals and the ghetto community.

824   _____, and Alan G. Hevesi, editors.   1969.   The
Politics of Urban Education.   New York: Praeger.

825   Goldhammer, Keith.   1955.   "Community Power Structure and School Board Membership."   American
School Board Journal 140 (March):   23-25.

826 _____. 1954. "The Roles of School District Offi-
      cials in Policy-Determination in an Oregon Commu-
      nity." Unpublished Ph.D. dissertation, University
      of Oregon.

827 Harper, Joe W. 1965. "A Study of Community Power
      Structure in Certain School Districts in the State of
      Texas and Its Influence on Bond Elections." Un-
      published Ed.D. dissertation, North Texas State Uni-
      versity.

828 Hill, William Barton. 1972. "Community Power Struc-
      tures and the Operation of a Selected School System."
      Unpublished Ed.D. dissertation, University of Massa-
      chusetts.

829 James, H. Thomas. 1967. "Politics and Community
      Decision-Making in Education." Review of Educa-
      tional Research 37 (October): 377-386.

830 Johns, Roe L., and Ralph Kimbrough. 1968. The
      Relationship of Socioeconomic Factors, Educational
      Leadership Patterns and Elements of Community
      Power Structure to Local School Policy. Washing-
      ton, D.C.: U.S. Department of Health, Education
      and Welfare, Office of Education, Bureau of Re-
      search.

831 Keisker, Larry Marvin. 1972. "A Description of the
      Informal Community Power Structure and the Rela-
      tionship of the Beliefs of the Influentials to the Ap-
      proval of the School District's Operating Tax Levy."
      Unpublished Ed.D. dissertation, Oklahoma State Uni-
      versity.

832 Kimbrough, Ralph B. 1964. Political Power and Edu-
      cational Decision Making. Chicago: Rand McNally.

833 Light, Kenneth Henry. 1964. "Community Power
      Structures and School District Reorganization." Un-
      published Ph.D. dissertation, University of Colorado.

834 Longstreth, James W. 1967. "The Relationship of Beliefs
      of Community Leaders, Teachers and Voters to School
      Fiscal Policy and Typology of Community Power Struc-
      ture." Unpublished Ph.D. dissertation, University of
      Florida.

835 Lutz, Frank W. 1965. "Power Structure and the
     School Board Decision-Making Process." Educa-
     tional Theory 15 (January): 19-25.

836 McDaniel, Ross Pat. 1973. "Community Influentials,
     Power Structures and Special Interest Groups and
     Their Influence on Individual Trustees in a Selected
     School District: A Case Study." Unpublished Ed. D.
     dissertation, University of Southern California.

837 Masotti, Louis H. 1967. Education and Politics in
     Suburbia: The New Trier Experience. Cleveland:
     Western Reserve University Press.

838 Masse, Berard. 1964. "A Comparison of the Relation-
     ship of Influentials to School in High and Low Finan-
     cial Support Communities." Unpublished Ph. D. dis-
     sertation, University of Michigan.

839 Merrill, Edward C. 1952. "Communication and De-
     cision-Making Related to the Administration of Edu-
     cation." Unpublished Ph. D. dissertation, George
     Peabody College for Teachers.

840 Miller, Jack A. 1970. "The Effects of the Power
     Structure Upon the Decision-Making Process of
     Boards of Education in Selected Missouri School
     Districts." Unpublished Ed. D. dissertation, Uni-
     versity of Missouri, Columbia.

841 Minar, David W. 1966. "The Community Basis of
     Conflict in School System Politics." American So-
     ciological Review 31 (December): 822-835.
          Minar found that conflict was handled better by
     communities which had more available skills (social
     statuses) in conflict management.

842 O'Donahue, John D. 1958. "The Green River Teachers' As-
     sociation: A Case Study of the Decision-Making Process."
     Unpublished Ed. D. dissertation, University of Oregon.

843 Proudfoot, Alexander. 1962. "A Study of the Socio-
     Economic Status of Influential School Board Members
     in Alberta as Related to Their Attitudes Toward Cer-
     tain Common Problems Confronting School Boards."
     Unpublished D. Ed. dissertation, University of Oregon.

844 Rosenberg, Morris. 1956. "Power and Desegregation."

Social Problems 3 (April): 215-223.

845 Rosenthal, Alan. 1961. "Community Leadership and
     Public School Politics: Two Case Studies." Unpub-
     lished Ph. D. dissertation, Princeton University.

846 _____, editor. 1969. Governing Education: A
     Reader on Politics, Power, and Public School Policy.
     New York: Doubleday.
          An examination of the politics and power struggles
     behind public education. The people involved in the edu-
     cational decision-making process are also examined.

847 Salisbury, Robert H. 1967. "Schools and Politics in
     the Big Cities." Harvard Educational Review 37
     (Summer): 408-424.

848 _____. 1966. "Urban Politics and Education." In
     Planning for a Nation of Cities, edited by Sam Bass
     Warner, Jr. Cambridge, Mass.: M. I. T. Press.
     268-284.

849 Scaggs, James Lewis. 1968. "Interaction Patterns of
     Superintendents with Community Power Systems in
     Twenty-Four Selected School Districts." Unpublished
     Ed. D. dissertation, University of Florida.

850 Scaggs, William F. 1963. "The Influentials in a Se-
     lected County School Administrative Unit: Their
     Norms and Resources." Unpublished Ed. D. disser-
     tation, University of Florida.

851 Schneider, Herbert H. 1969. "A Comparative Study of
     Political Power and Educational Decision-Making in
     Two Small School Districts." Unpublished Ph. D. dis-
     sertation, Ohio State University.

852 Seeker, William A. 1969. "Power Structure and
     School Bond Elections." Unpublished Ph. D. disser-
     tation, Texas A. & M. University.

853 Shibles, Mark R. 1968. "Community Power Structures
     and District School Organization Relationships: An
     Exploratory Analysis of Input Functions." Unpub-
     lished Ph. D. dissertation, Cornell University.

854 Spiess, John A. 1967. "Community Power Structure
     and Influence: Relationships to Educational

Administration." Unpublished Ph. D. dissertation,
University of Iowa.

855 Steinert, Raymond. 1971. "Community Power Structure in Relation to Implementation of Controversial
Issue Programs in Nebraska Elementary Schools."
Unpublished Ed. D. dissertation, University of Nebraska.

856 Thomas, Michael P., Jr. 1966. Community Governance and the School Board: A Case Study. Austin,
Texas: Institute of Public Affairs, No. 71, University of Texas.

857 Webb, Harold V. 1956. Community Power Structure
Related to School Administration. Laramie, Wy.:
University of Wyoming Press.

858 Willie, Charles V. 1968. "New Perspectives in
School-Community Relationships." Journal of Negro
Education 37 (Summer): 220-226.

859 Wilson, L. Craig. 1952. "Community Power Pressure
and Control in Relation to Education in a Selected
County." Unpublished Ph. D. dissertation, George
Peabody College for Teachers.

860 Zimmer, Basil G., and Amos H. Hawley. 1968.
Metropolitan Area Schools: Resistance to District
Reorganization. Beverly Hills, Cal.: Sage Publica-
tions.

861 _____, and _____. 1967. "Opinions on School
District Reorganization in Metropolitan Areas: A
Comparative Analysis of the Views of Citizens and
Officials in Central City and Suburban Areas."
Southwestern Social Science Quarterly 48 (December):
311-324.
    Suburban residents were more opposed to change
than city residents while suburban officials were
more in favor of change than city officials.

862 _____, and _____. 1967. "Opinions on School
District Reorganization in Metropolitan Areas: A
Comparative Analysis of the Views of Citizens and
Officials in Central City and Suburban Areas." Un-
published paper read at the meeting of the Society
for the Study of Social Problems.

Urban Planning and Development

863 Aiken, Michael, and Robert R. Alford. 1970. "Community Structure and Innovation: The Case of Public
Housing." American Political Science Review 64
(September): 843-864.
    Innovation in housing was determined by structural
differentiation, the accumulation of experience and information, and the stability and extensiveness of in-
terorganizational networks in communities.

864 _____, and _____. "Community Structure and
Innovation: The Case of Urban Renewal." American
Sociological Review 35 (August): 650-664.
    A model of interorganizational networks and struc-
tural requisites for effecting decisions in a community
was developed.

865 Akenson, Curtis Burcette. 1962. "Selected Facets of
Community Influence on Political Power in the Redevelopment of the Minneapolis Lower Loop." Unpublished Ph. D. dissertation, University of Minne-
sota.

866 Ashley, Thomas J. 1962. "Power and Politics in Community Planning: An Empirical Analysis of Four Selected Policy Decisions Made in Anaheim, California
Between 1945-1960." Unpublished Ph. D. dissertation,
Claremont Graduate School and University Center.

867 Auerbach, Arnold J. 1961. "The Pattern of Community Leadership in Urban Redevelopment: A Pittsburgh Profile." Unpublished Ph. D. dissertation,
University of Pittsburgh.

868 Bellush, Jewell, and Murray Hausknecht, editors. 1967.
Urban Renewal: People, Politics and Planning. New
York: Doubleday.
    A collection of papers stressing the political de-
cision-making process and how it affects urban renewal. The problems of government leadership and
citizen participation in the urban renewal decision-
making process are central topics.

869 Bouma, Donald H. 1952. "An Analysis of the Social
Power Position of the Real Estate Board in Grand
Rapids, Michigan." Unpublished Ph. D. dissertation,
Michigan State College.

870 _____. 1962. "The Legitimation of the Social
   Power Position of a Real Estate Board." American
   Journal of Economics and Sociology 21 (October):
   383-392.

871 Brown, Bernard. 1967. "Municipal Finances and An-
   nexation: A Case Study of Post-War Houston."
   Southwestern Social Science Quarterly 48 (December):
   339-351.

872 Burby, Raymond Joseph III. 1968. "Planning and Poli-
   tics: Toward a Model of Planning-Related Policy
   Outputs in American Local Government." Unpublished
   Ph.D. dissertation, University of North Carolina.

873 Burke, Edmund M. 1967. "The Search for Authority
   in Planning." Social Service Review 41 (September):
   250-260.

874 Cafiero, S. 1969. "Parteciparione e Potere Nell'Esper-
   ienza Italiana di Sviluppo Communitario" [Participa-
   tion and Power in the Italian Experience of Community Development]. International Review of Community Development 21-22 (December): 31-36.

875 Davies, James C., III. 1963. Neighborhood Groups
   and Urban Renewal. New York: Columbia University Press.

876 Duggar, George S. 1961. "The Relation of Local
   Government Structure to Urban Renewal." Law and
   Contemporary Problems 26 (Winter): 49-69.

877 Hawley, Amos H. 1963. "Community Power and Urban Renewal Success." American Journal of Sociology
   68 (January): 422-431.
      Hawley suggests that collective action success,
   i.e., urban renewal, is dependent on the concentration of power in a city. In this article, Hawley developed his 'MPO ratio' to measure power concentration. It is a purely demographic measure con-
   sisting of the ratio of persons in occupations classified as managers, proprietors, or officials to all
   other occupations. Hawley interpreted a low ratio
   as indicating a concentration of power. Subsequently,
   however, Aiken and others have shown that the 'MPO
   ratio' correlated with the opposite pattern suggested

by Hawley, basing their conclusions on the results of
correlating the 'MPO ratio' with case studies of actual decisions.

878 Kaplan, Harold. 1963. Urban Renewal Politics. New
      York: Columbia University Press.

879 Long, Norton. 1959. "Planning and Politics in Urban
      Development. " Journal of the American Institute of
      Planners 25 (November): 167-169.
        Long argues that the planner should abandon his
      role strictly as a planner and he should become
      more involved in local politics because of the politi-
      cal nature of his work.

880 Meyerson, Martin, and Edward Banfield. 1955. Poli-
      tics, Planning, and Public Interest. Glencoe, Ill. :
      The Free Press.

881 Plant, H. T. 1964. "Local Government and Commu-
      nity Development in Rural Areas of Papua and New
      Guinea. " Journal of Local Administration Overseas
      3 (April): 107-113.

882 Rabinovitz, Francine F. 1969. City Politics and Plan-
      ning. New York: Atherton Press.

883 _____. 1967. "Politics, Personality, and Planning. "
      Public Administration Review 27 (March): 18-24.

884 Ranney, Gerald. 1969. Planning and Politics in the
      Metropolis. Columbus: Charles E. Merrill.

885 Rossi, Peter H. and Robert Dentler. 1961. Politics
      of Urban Renewal. Glencoe, Ill. : The Free Press.

886 Straits, Bruce C. 1965. "Community Adoption and
      Implementation of Urban Renewal. " American Jour-
      nal of Sociology 71 (July): 77-82.
        Straits found only a very slight relationship be-
      tween Hawley's MPO ratio and urban renewal prog-
      ress.

887 Warren, Roland L. 1969. "Model Cities First Round:
      Politics, Planning, and Participation. " Journal of
      the American Institute of Planners 15 (July): 245-
      252.

888 Wilson, James Q. 1963. "Planning and Politics: Citi-
     zen Participation in Urban Renewal." Journal of the
     American Institute of Planners 34 (November): 242-
     249.
          Citizen participation in urban renewal has become
     an integral part of local politics. Community organ-
     izations have become powerful enough to have grow-
     ing consequences for big city mayors.

889 Wingfield, C. J. 1963. "Power Structure and Deci-
     sion-Making in City Planning." Public Administra-
     tion Review 23 (June): 74-80.
          Wingfield stresses the educational function that the
     planner must perform in order to bring planning de-
     cisions in line with public policy.

Minority Groups

890 Abbott, Arnold Peter. 1965. "A Study of Power Struc-
     ture and the Negro Sub-Community." Unpublished
     M. A. thesis, University of Pennsylvania.

891 Altshuler, Alan A. 1970. Community Control: The
     Black Demand for Participation in Large American
     Cities. New York: Pegasus.

892 Barth, Ernest A. T. , and Baha Abu-Laban. 1959.
     "Power Structure and the Negro Sub-Community."
     American Sociological Review 24 (February): 69-
     76.

893 Bellush, Jewell, and Stephen M. David, editors. 1971.
     Race and Politics in New York City: Five Studies
     in Policy-Making. New York: Praeger.

894 Burgess, M. Elaine. 1962. Negro Leadership in a
     Southern City. Chapel Hill: University of North
     Carolina Press.
          Because of new federal laws and the 1954 Supreme
     Court decision, the power structure of Crescent City
     has expanded to include the Negro sub-community
     leaders. The Negro leaders have effectively mobilized
     their resources for the attainment of sub-community
     goals.

895 Coleman, James. 1971. Resources for Social Change.

New York: John Wiley & Sons.

896   Danzger, M. Herbert.   1968.   "Civil Rights Conflict
       and Community Power Structure."   Unpublished
       Ph.D. dissertation, Columbia University.

897   Hadden, Jeffrey K., Louis H. Masotti, and Victor
       Thiessen.   1968.   "The Making of Negro Mayors,
       1967."   Transaction 5 (January-February):   21-30.

898   Harvey, Clyde.   1971.   "A Case Study of a Black Com-
       munity's Leadership Structure in a Rural Southeast
       Georgia County."   Unpublished Ph.D. dissertation,
       University of Georgia.

899   Holloway, Harry.   1968.   "Negro Political Strategy:
       Coalition or Independent Power Politics?"   Social
       Science Quarterly 49 (December):   534-547.

900   Killian, Lewis M.   1965.   "Community Structure and
       the Role of the Negro Leader-Agent."   Sociological
       Inquiry 35 (Winter):   69-79.
          A study of the Negro leader-agent and his rela-
       tionships to the black and white sub-communities.

901   _____, and Charles U. Smith.   1960.   "Negro Pro-
       test Leaders in a Southern Community."   Social
       Forces 38 (March):   253-257.
          An examination of the changes in Negro leader-
       ship in Tallahassee during the bus boycott.   The
       new leaders were more permanent and better able
       to change the course of race relations there.

902   Kramer, John, and Ingo Walter.   1968.   "Politics in
       an All-Negro City."   Urban Affairs Quarterly 4
       (September):   65-87.

903   McKee, James.   1958-59.   "Community Power and
       Strategies in Race Relations: Some Critical Obser-
       vations."   Social Problems 6 (Winter):   41-51.

904   Ottenberg, S.   1959.   "Leadership and Change in a
       Coastal Georgia Negro Community."   Phylon 20
       (March):   7-18.

905   Parenton, Vernon J., and Roland J. Pellegrin.   1956.
       "Social Structure and Leadership Factors in a Negro

Community in South Louisiana." <u>Phylon</u> 17 (March): 74-78.

906 Pfautz, Harold W. 1962. "The Power Structure of the Negro Sub-Community: A Case Study and a Comparative View." <u>Phylon</u> 23 (Summer): 156-166.
The community leaders in the Negro sub-community. Conflicts occurred between the old and young sub-community leaders.

907 _____, Harry C. Huguley, and John W. McClain, Jr. 1973. "Changes in Reputed Black Community Leadership: 1962-1972, A Case Study." Unpublished paper presented at the meeting of the American Sociological Association.

908 _____, and John W. McClain, Jr. 1971. "The Power Structure of a Black Subcommunity: A Replicated Case Study." Unpublished paper presented at the meeting of the Eastern Sociological Society.

909 Thompson, Daniel. 1963. <u>The Negro Leadership Class</u>. Englewood Cliffs, N. J.: Prentice-Hall.
Thompson elaborated on Hunter's thesis and attempted to find the place of Negro leadership in New Orleans in the decision-making process. He concluded that the power structure of New Orleans was similar to the power structure that Hunter found in Atlanta. That is, none of the leaders of the Negro community were involved in the top echelons of power in the community.

910 Walker, Jack L. 1963. "Protest and Negotiation: A Case Study of Negro Leadership in Atlanta." <u>Midwest Journal of Political Science</u> 7 (May): 99-124.

911 Wilson, James Q. 1959. "Negro Leaders in Chicago." Unpublished Ph. D. dissertation, University of Chicago.

912 _____. 1960. <u>Negro Politics: The Search for Leadership</u>. Glencoe, Ill.: The Free Press.

Labor

913 Belknap, George, and John Bunzel. 1958. "The Trade Union in the Political Community." <u>PROD</u> 2 (September): 3-6

914 Form, William H. 1959. "Organized Labor's Place in
the Community Power Structure." Industrial and
Labor Relations Review 12 (July): 526-539.

915 _____, and Warren L. Sauer. 1963. "Labor and
Community Influentials: A Comparative Study of Participation and Imagery." Industrial and Labor Relations Review 17 (October): 3-19.

916 _____, and _____. 1960. "Organized Labor's
Image of Community Power Structure." Social Forces
38 (May): 332-341.
   Form and Sauer found that while labor saw the
power structure in the hands of management, it did
see itself within the power structure also. Labor
did feel excluded from the initiation of projects, but
did insist that it has a powerful voice when it got
involved. The goals of local government were seen
as identical between labor and management.

917 Hudson, James R. 1965. "Power With Low Prestige:
A Study of Labor Unions in a Dependent Community."
Unpublished Ph.D. dissertation, University of Michi-
gan.

918 Lyons, Schley R. 1969. "Labor in City Politics."
Social Science Quarterly 49 (March): 816-828.

919 McKee, James B. 1953. "Organized Labor and Community Decision-Making: A Study in the Sociology
of Power." Unpublished Ph.D. dissertation, University of Wisconsin.

920 Sauer, Warren L. 1960. "Labor-Business Images of
Community Power: Convergences and Divergences."
Unpublished Ph.D. dissertation, Michigan State Uni-
versity.

Press and Mass Media

921 Christenso, Reo M. 1959. "The Power of the Press:
The Case of 'The Toledo Blade'." Midwest Journal
of Political Science 3 (August): 227-240.

922 Edelstein, Alex S., and J. Blaine Schulz. 1964. "The
Leadership of the Weekly Newspaper as Seen by

Community Leaders: A Sociological Perspective."
In People, Society, and Mass Communications, edited
by Lewis A. Dexter and David Manning White.
Glencoe, Ill.: The Free Press. 221-238.

923 _____, and _____. 1963. "The Weekly Newspaper's Leadership Role as Seen by Community
Leaders." Journalism Quarterly 40 (Autumn): 565-
574.

924 Ehrlich, Howard J., and M. L. Bauer. 1965. "Newspaper Citation and Reputation for Community Leadership." American Sociological Review 30 (June):
411-415.
    It was found that reputational community leaders
appeared with frequency in the local press. The
frequency of these citations was stable across all
the local newspapers. Ehrlich and Bauer also found
a high correlation between reputations for leadership,
holding political office and newspaper citation.

925 Goldstein, Marshall N., and Robert S. Cahill. 1964.
"Mass Media and Community Politics." In The
Politics of Education in the Local Community, edited
by Robert S. Cahill and Stephen Hencley. Danville,
Ill.: Interstate Printers & Publishers. 163-188.

926 Hvistendahl, J. K. 1970. "Publisher's Power: Functional or Dysfunctional?" Journalism Quarterly 47
(Autumn): 472-478.
    It was found that community power status may be
functional in relation to the performance of the duties
of editors of large papers. The opposite was found
for editors of small papers.

927 Remmenga, Alvin J. 1961. "Has the Press Lost Its
Influence in Local Affairs?" In Urban Government:
A Reader in Administration and Politics, edited by
Edward C. Banfield. Glencoe, Ill.: The Free
Press. 256-260.

928 Sim, John Cameron. 1967. "Community Newspaper
Leadership: More Real Than Apparent?" Journalism
Quarterly 44 (Summer): 276-280.
    A review of power structure literature revealed
that newspaper editors and publishers are rarely
identified as powerful figures in community decision-

making. Sims finds this paradoxical since newspapers traditionally have been molders of community
opinion. He concluded, because of this, that effective techniques for identifying community influentials
have yet to be devised.

929 Thorp, Robert Kent. 1963. "The Role of the Daily
     Newspaper Publisher in the Community Power Struc-
     ture." Unpublished Ph. D. dissertation, State Uni-
     versity of Iowa.

Voluntary Associations

930 Allcock, John B. 1968. "Voluntary Associations and
     the Structure of Power." Sociological Review 16
     (March): 59-82.
         A study of the relations between the broadcasting
     organizations and the Christian churches in the com-
     munity revealed a high level of integration of the
     elite in both groups. It was suggested that this high
     level of integration threatened traditional pluralist
     structure in the community.

931 Drake, George F. 1970. "Elites and Voluntary Asso-
     ciations: A Study of Community Power in Manizabes,
     Colombia." Unpublished Ph. D. dissertation, Univer-
     sity of Wisconsin.

932 Ehrlich, Howard J. 1968. "Voluntary Associations and
     Community Decision-Making--A Paradigm." Research
     Reports in Social Science 2 (Spring): 19-31.

933 Eitzen, D. Stanley. 1966. "A Study of the Voluntary
     Association Memberships of Formal Community
     Leaders." Unpublished master's thesis, University
     of Kansas.

934 _____, and Charles K. Warriner. 1967. "Voluntary
     Association Memberships: A Comparison of Formal
     and Informal Community Leaders." Kansas Journal
     of Sociology 3 (Fall): 147-152.

935 Laskin, Richard. 1962. Leadership of Voluntary Or-
     ganizations in a Saskatchewan Town. Saskatoon:
     Centre for Community Studies.

936 Newton, K. 1973. "Pluralistic Theory and the Partici-
      pation of Voluntary Organizations in Community Poli-
      tics." Unpublished paper presented at the meeting
      of the American Sociological Association.

937 Payne, Raymond. 1954. "An Approach to the Study of
      Relative Prestige of Formal Organizations." Social
      Forces 32 (March): 244-247.

938 Rose, Arnold. 1952. "Power Distribution in the Com-
      munity Through Voluntary Associations." In Prob-
      lems in Social Psychology, edited by J. W. Julett
      and Ross Stagner. Urbana: University of Illinois
      Press. 74-83.

939 Sallach, David L. 1973. "Voluntary Associations and
      Power: A Re-Assessment." Unpublished paper pre-
      sented at the meeting of the American Sociological
      Association.

Poverty and Welfare

940 Bachrach, Peter. 1970. "A Power Analysis: The
      Shaping of Antipoverty Policy in Baltimore."
      Public Policy 18 (Winter): 155-186.

941 _____. 1969. "A Power Analysis: The Shaping of
      Antipoverty Policy in Baltimore." Unpublished paper
      presented at the meeting of the American Political
      Science Association.

942 Butler, Edgar W., and Hallowell Pope. 1966. "Com-
      munity Power Structures, Industrialization and Public
      Welfare Programs." Unpublished paper presented at
      the meeting of the American Sociological Association.

943 Mackinnon, F. R. 1960. "Local Government and Wel-
      fare." Canadian Public Administration 3 (March):
      31-41.

944 Paulson, Wayne, Edgar W. Butler, and Hallowell Pope.
      1969. "Community Power and Public Welfare."
      American Journal of Economics and Sociology 28
      (January): 17-27.

945 Sheak, Robert, et al. 1971. "The Power Elite and

Welfare in St. Louis." Unpublished paper presented
at the meeting of the American Sociological Association.

946 Vinton, Dennis A. 1969. "The Relationship Between
the Power Structure and Parks and Recreation in a
Large Urban Community." Unpublished Re.D. dissertation, Indiana University.

947 Wachtel, Dawn Day. 1968. "Structures of Community
and Strategies for Organization." Social Work 13
(January): 85-91.

948 Willie, Charles V. 1965. "Community Leadership in
the Voluntary Health and Welfare System." In
Applied Sociology: Opportunities and Problems,
edited by Alvin Gouldner and S. M. Miller. New
York: The Free Press. 207-214.

949 Zurcher, Louis A. 1967. "Functional Marginality:
Dynamics of a Poverty Intervention Organization."
Southwestern Social Science Quarterly 48 (December):
411-421.

950 _____. 1966. "Functional Marginality: Dynamics
of a Poverty Intervention Organization." Unpublished
paper presented at the meeting of the Society for the
Study of Social Problems.

Health

951 Belknap, Ivan, and John Steinle. 1963. The Community and Its Hospitals. Syracuse, New York: Syracuse University Press.

952 Blankenship, L. Vaughn, and Ray H. Elling. 1962.
"Organizational Support and Community Power Structure: The Hospital." Journal of Health and Human
Behavior 3 (Winter): 257-268.
Financial support for hospital programs was related to the hospital's ties with the community power
structure. However, short-run community programs
were not dependent on support from the community
power structure.

953 Elling, Ray. 1968. "Power Structure in Health."

Milbank Memorial Fund Quarterly 46 (January): 119-
143.
Power was analyzed in terms of an effective and
comprehensive plan to coordinate health services
within a region.

954   Erbe, William. 1971. "The Changing Community Role
of Health Professionals." Unpublished paper presented at the meeting of the Society for the Study of
Social Problems.

955   Lee, Ollie J. 1969. "Community Leaders and Their
Involvement in the Health System of a Metropolitan
Community." Unpublished Ph.D. dissertation, Uni-
versity of Pittsburgh.

956   Miller, Paul A. 1953. Community Health Action.
East Lansing: Michigan State University Press.

957   _____. 1954. "A Comparative Analysis of the
Decision Process: Community Organization Toward
Major Health Goals." Unpublished Ph.D. disser-
tation, Michigan State University.

958   Palumbo, Dennis J., and Oliver P. Williams. 1967.
"Predictors of Public Policy: The Case of Local
Public Health." Urban Affairs Quarterly 2 (June):
75-93.

959   Prince, Julius S. 1958. "The Health Officer and Community Power Groups." Health Education Monographs
No. 2: 16-31.

960   Willie, Charles V. 1961. "A Success Story of Community Action." Nursing Outlook 9 (January): 19-
21.

Religion

961   Danzger, M. Herbert. 1962. "The Place of the Religious Elite in the Community Power Structure." Unpublished M.A. thesis, Columbia University.

962   Dolbeare, Kenneth M., and Phillip E. Hammond. 1971.
Prayers and Politics: From Court Policy to Local
Practice. Chicago: University of Chicago Press.

A study of the response of local community governments in five midwestern communities to the Supreme Court decision barring prayers in public schools. The local elites found various ways of permitting noncompliance with the ruling.

963 Mitchell, John B. , Eldon C. Schriner, and Edward D.
     LaFontaine. 1970. "Influentials and the Church in
     Small Communities. " Review of Religious Research
     11 (Spring): 192-196.
          In small communities, the church has great potential for influencing community decision-making.

964 _____, _____, and _____. 1963. "In Small
     Communities, Are Churches Still Important Influences ?" Ohio Report 53 (Nov. -Dec.): 85-87.

965 Roseman, Kenneth. 1969. "Power in a Midwestern
     Jewish Community. " American Jewish Archives 21
     (April): 57-83.

RURAL STUDIES

966 Andrews, Wade D. 1956. "Some Correlates of Rural
     Leadership and Social Power Among Intercommunity
     Leaders. " Unpublished Ph. D. dissertation, Michigan
     State University.

967 Beal, George M. , Paul Yarbrough, Gerald E. Klonglan,
     and Joe M. Bohlen. 1964. Social Action in Civil
     Defense. Ames: Rural Sociology Report No. 34,
     Department of Economics and Sociology, Iowa State
     University of Science and Technology.

968 Bensman, Joseph. 1959. "Small Town in Mass Society:
     Class, Power, Religion in a Rural Community. " Unpublished Ph. D. dissertation, Columbia University.

969 Bohlen, Joe M. , George M. Beal, Gerald E. Klonglan,
     and John L. Tait. 1964. Community Power Structure and Civil Defense. Ames: Rural Sociology Report No. 35, Department of Economics and Sociology,
     Iowa State University of Science and Technology.

970 Bonser, H. J. , R. G. Milk, and C. E. Alred. 1942.

Local Leadership in Rural Communities of Kimberlin
County, Tennessee. Monograph No. 144, Tennessee
Agricultural Experiment Station, Agricultural Economy
and Rural Sociology Department.

971 Carpenter, D. B. 1951. "Some Factors Associated
With Influence Positions in the Associational Structure of a Rural Community." Unpublished Ph. D.
dissertation, University of Washington.

972 Freeman, Charles M. 1956. "Leadership in Rural
Community Action: A Study of Decision Making."
Unpublished Ph. D. dissertation. North Carolina
State University, Raleigh.

973 _____, and Selz C. Mayo. 1957. "Decision-Makers
in Rural Community Action." Social Forces 35
(May): 319-322.
         Freeman and Mayo found that the upper-level
leaders were in contact with lower-level leaders
and involved in low-cost as well as high-cost decisions.

974 Gagan, R. J. 1969. "Pluralism and Community Struc-
ture: A Comparative Analysis of Rural Centers in
New York State." Unpublished Ph. D. dissertation,
Cornell University.

975 Given, C. William, and John B. Mitchell. 1971. Community Power Structure: A Methodological Analysis
and Comparison. Wooster: Research Bulletin 1046,
Ohio Agricultural Research and Development Center.

976 Kammeyer, Kenneth. 1962. "A Comparative Study of
Decision Making in Rural Communities." Rural
Sociology 27 (September): 294-302.
         A comparison of ecological and demographic fac-
tors in rural community decision-making in one hun-
dred and ten communities. Opposition to reorganization of high schools increased as communities get
smaller. Kammeyer suggests that this may be due
to the citizen's fear that the community may collapse
if they lose their high school.

977 Mitchell, John B. , and Ralph W. Moore. 1965. "Small
Town Power Structure." Journal of Cooperative Extension 3 (Winter): 213-218.

A study of the power structure of a small Ohio town. It was found that the most likely way of penetrating the power structure was through marriage and not through economic gains or economic prestige.

978 Mleczko, Franciszek Wiktor. 1967. "Wladza Lokalna w Srodowisku Wiejskim" [Local Authority in the Rural Environment]. Studia Socjologiczno Polityczne 23: 95-105.

979 Oommen, T. K. 1969. "Political Leadership in Rural India: Image and Reality." Asian Survey 9 (July): 515-521.

980 _____. 1970. "Rural Community Power Structure in India." Social Forces 49 (December): 226-239.
        A study of four villages in India found that community size was not an important factor in power dispersion. A weakening of kinship solidarity may facilitate wider political participation. The greater the heterogeneity of the community, the greater the possibility of the use of competing power centers. An increase in literacy brings with it an increase in political consciousness and participation.

981 Payne, Raymond. 1963. "Leadership and Perception of Change in a Village Confronted With Urbanism." Social Forces 41 (March): 264-269.
        Leaders of rural villages expected change and had definite ideas on how it should take place. They would prefer these changes many times and would prefer to assist in the changes they prefer than be in positions of leadership during the expected change.

982 Perkins, Larry Manson. 1963. "Leadership in a New York Rural Community." Unpublished D. S. S. dissertation, Syracuse University.

983 Powers, Ronald Clair. 1963. "Social Power in a Rural Community." Unpublished Ph. D. dissertation, Iowa State University of Science and Technology.

984 Robins, J. W. 1961. "Developments in Rural Local Government in Nyasaland." Journal of African Administration 13 (July): 148-157.

985 Rubenstein, Dan, and Barry Gordon. 1973. "The

Socially Constructive Aspects of Outside Agents in
Community Decision Making in a Rural Area of West
Virginia." Unpublished paper presented at the meet-
ing of the American Sociological Association.

986 Speight, John F.   1971. "Commentary on Oommen's
     'Rural Community Power Structure in India'." Social
     Forces 50 (December): 261.

987 Subramaniam, K. S.   1970. "Local Authorities in
     Rural India." Quarterly Journal of the Local Self-
     Government Institute 40 (April-June): 317-333.

988 Tait, John L.   1964. "Social Power in a Rural Social
     System." Unpublished M.S. thesis, Iowa State
     University of Science and Technology.

989 Young, James N. , and Selz C. Mayo.   1959. "Mani-
     fest and Latent Participators in Rural Community
     Action Programs." Social Forces 38 (December):
     140-145.
        Only a small proportion of community residents
     participated in community affairs at more than a
     minimal level.

4

COMPARATIVE COMMUNITY POWER STUDIES

DISCUSSIONS

990 Aiken, Michael, and Robert R. Alford. 1970. "Comparative Urban Research and Community Decision-Making." The New Atlantis 1 (Winter): 85-110.

991 Alford, Robert R. 1967. "The Comparative Study of Urban Politics." In Urban Research and Policy Planning, edited by Leo F. Schnore and Henry Fagin. Beverly Hills, Cal.: Sage Publications. 263-302.

992 Clark, Terry N. 1973. "Community Autonomy in the National System: Federalism, Localism, and Decentralization." In Comparative Community Politics, edited by Terry N. Clark. Beverly Hills, Cal.: Sage Publications.

993 _____, editor. 1968. Community Structure and Decision-Making: Comparative Analyses. San Francisco: Chandler Pub. Co.

994 _____. 1966. "Comparability in Community Research." Unpublished paper presented at the meeting of the International Sociological Association.

995 _____, editor. 1973. Comparative Community Politics. Beverly Hills, Cal.: Sage Publications.

996 Coutler, Phillip B. 1970. "Comparative Community Politics & Public Policy." Polity 3 (Fall): 22-43.

997 Downes, Bryan T., and Timothy Hennessey. 1969. "Theory and Concept Formation in the Comparative Study of Urban Politics: Problems of Process and

Change." Unpublished paper presented at the meeting of the American Political Science Association.

998 Eisenstadt, S. N. 1965. "Bureaucracy, Bureaucrati-
zation, Markets and Power Structure." In Essays
in Comparative Institutions, edited by S. N. Eisenstadt. New York: John Wiley & Sons. 177-215.

999 Griswold, Leonard E. 1956. "The Community as a
Social System: A Study in Comparative Analysis."
Unpublished Ph. D. dissertation, University of Ken-
tucky.

1000 Hennessey, Timothy M. 1970. "Problems in Concept
Formation: The Ethos 'Theory' and the Compara-
tive Study of Urban Politics." Midwest Journal of
Political Science 14 (November): 537-564.
A critique of concepts that have been used in the
study of urban politics, especially Banfield and
Wilson's ethos theory. Hennessey argues that ethos
theory is poorly suited for comparative research.

1001 Jambrek, Peter. 1969. "Some Methodological Problems of Cross-National Comparison of Community
Decision-Making: The Case of Yugoslavia and the
U. S." Unpublished paper presented at the meeting
of the International Conference on Community Decision-Making, Italy.

1002 Kesselman, Mark. 1970. "Research Choices in Comparative Local Politics." The New Atlantis 1 (Winter): 48-64.

1003 _____. 1973. "Research Perspectives in Comparative Local Politics: Reflections on Theory and
Notes on the French Case." In Comparative Community Politics, edited by Terry N. Clark. Beverly Hills, Cal. : Sage Publications.

1004 _____. 1972. "Research Perspectives in Comparative Urban Politics: Pitfalls and Prospects." Comparative Urban Research 1 (Spring): 10-30.
Kesselman opposes studying community power in
other than American communities using research
techniques developed in American studies. He argues that communities outside the United States are
more integrated with wider political processes than

American communities. Therefore, different kinds
of questions must be examined in non-American
communities.

1005 _____, and Donald B. Rosenthal. 1972. "Local
Power and Comparative Politics: Notes Toward
the Study of Comparative Local Politics." Unpublished paper presented at the meeting of the American Political Science Association.
Kesselman and Rosenthal suggest some dimensions for analysis in future comparative community
power studies. These dimensions are 'localism'
and its relationship with the national political culture, the structural arrangements of local governance, and localistic political processes and their
effects on local political actors.

1006 Kuroda, Yasumasa. 1971. "A Comparative Analysis
of Local Politics in Asia: Methodological and
Theoretical Concerns." Il Politico 36 (June): 239-
267.
A review of the studies of comparative community politics in Asia and the United States. Kuroda
suggests new strategies and methodologies that
could be used in future studies.

1007 _____. 1970. "A Comparative Study of Local Politics in Asia: A Review and Methodological Considerations." Unpublished paper presented at the
meeting of the International Political Science Association.

1008 Milbrath, Lester W. 1970. "A Paradigm for the
Comparative Study of Local Politics." Unpublished
paper presented at the meeting of the International
Political Science Association.

1009 Ostrowski, Krysztoff, and Henry Teune. 1973. "Local Political Systems and General Social Processes."
In Comparative Community Politics, edited by
Terry N. Clark. Beverly Hills, Cal.: Sage Publications.

1010 Rejai, Mostafa. 1969. "Toward the Comparative
Study of Political Decision-Makers." Comparative
Political Studies 2 (October): 349-360.

1011   Rogers, David. 1962. "Community Political Systems:
       A Framework and Hypothesis for Comparative
       Studies." In Current Trends in Comparative
       Studies, edited by Bert Swanson. Kansas City,
       Mo.: Community Studies. 31-48.

1012   Swanson, Bert E., editor. 1962. Current Trends in
       Comparative Community Studies. Kansas City,
       Mo.: Community Studies.

1013   Tilly, Charles. 1973. "The Chaos of the Living
       City." In Comparative Community Politics, edited
       by Terry N. Clark. Beverly Hills, Cal.: Sage
       Publications.

1014   Wiatr, J. 1971. "Comparative Study of Local Poli-
       tics: Post-Congress Reflections. Il Politico 36
       (December): 647-659.

1015   Williams, Oliver P., and Charles R. Adrian. 1961.
       "A Typology for Comparative Local Government."
       Midwest Journal of Political Science 5 (May): 150-
       164.

1016   Zink, Harold, editor. 1956. "Selected Materials for
       a Comparative Study of Local Government." Amer-
       ican Political Science Review 50 (December): 1107-
       1133.

COMPARATIVE STUDIES

1017   Adrian, Charles. 1958. "Leadership and Decision-
       Making in Manager Cities: A Study of Three Com-
       munities." Public Administration Review 18 (Sum-
       mer): 208-213.

1018   Agger, Robert, Daniel Goldrich, and Bert Swanson.
       1959. "Political Influence Structures in Four Com-
       munities." Unpublished paper presented at the
       meeting of the American Sociological Association.

1019   _____, _____, and _____. 1964. The Rulers
       and the Ruled: Political Power and Impotence in
       American Communities. New York: John Wiley &
       Sons.

In a study of four communities, the authors did
not find the 'ideal type' of power structure--the
consensual mass. In three of the four communities,
the distribution of power had shifted from mass to
elite. Their stress on values and political culture
has been important for subsequent work, as well as
the emphasis on comparisons across communities.

1020 Aiken, Michael. 1969. "Community Power and Community Mobilization." Annals of the American
Academy of Political and Social Science 385
(September): 76-88.
Aiken found that cities that have power structures that are 'diffuse' or decentralized have
greater participation in community programs such
as anti-poverty activities and urban renewal.

1021 _____, and Robert R. Alford. 1973. "Community
Structure and Innovation: Public Housing, Urban
Renewal and the War on Poverty." In Comparative
Community Politics, edited by Terry N. Clark.
Beverly Hills, Cal.: Sage Publications.

1022 Alford, Robert R. 1969. "Bureaucracy and Participation in Four Wisconsin Cities." Urban Affairs
Quarterly 5 (September): 5-30.

1023 _____, in collaboration with Harry M. Scoble.
1969. Bureaucracy and Participation: Political
Cultures in Four Wisconsin Cities. Chicago:
Rand McNally.

1024 Allegrucci, Robert L. 1969. "An Analysis of the
Social Structure and Ideological Sources of Elitism:
A Comparative Study of Community Power." Unpublished Ph.D. dissertation, University of Mis-
souri, Columbia.

1025 Anton, Thomas J. 1973. "Environment, Culture and
Structure in the Changing Politics of Swedish Mu-
nicipalities." In Comparative Community Politics,
edited by Terry N. Clark. Beverly Hills, Cal.:
Sage Publications.

1026 Banfield, Edward C. 1965. Big City Politics. New
York: Random House.
A comparison of nine political systems and how

they function.   The areas of government organization, elections, interest groups, power influentials,
and decision-making were examined in each of nine
large American cities.   This volume is a brief
summary of a major program of comparative case
studies undertaken by Banfield and his associates
at the Joint Center for Urban Studies, Harvard-
M. I. T.   The case studies themselves are available
in mimeographed form in many of the larger American university libraries.   They are more useful
than many case studies as they were undertaken
from a common perspective.   They are especially
illuminating for such matters as mayoral elections,
city council and interest group politics, the role of
major local actors (business, newspapers, labor,
etc.), and the patterns of patronage in different cities.

1027   Barth, Ernest A. T.   1963.   "Air Force Base-Host
        Community Relations: A Study in Community
        Typology. " Social Forces 41 (March): 260-264.
           Barth developed two typologies from the com-
        parative study of 10 Air Force-host communities.
        One typology concerned community process and one
        typology concerned community structure.

1028   _____. 1961. "Community Influence Systems: Struc-
        ture and Change. " Social Forces 40 (October): 58-63.
           In a comparative study of six communities, Barth
        found that community influence systems vary in their
        shape from highly structured to virtually no struc-
        ture of influence.   Barth also found that population
        growth was a major determinant of the shape of the
        influence system.

1029   Blankenship, L. Vaughn.   1962.   "Organizational Sup-
        port and Community Leadership in Two New York
        State Communities. " Unpublished Ph. D. disserta-
        tion, Cornell University.
           The community owned hospitals in two New York
        communities were examined to delineate their support
        from the communities.   Particularly important was
        the examination of leadership ties to the hospitals.

1030   Bohlen, Joe M. , George M. Beal, Gerald E. Klonglan,
        and John L. Tait.   1967.   A Comparative Analysis
        of Community Power Structures.   Ames: Rural
        Sociology Report No. 50, Department of Sociology
        and Anthropology, Iowa State University.

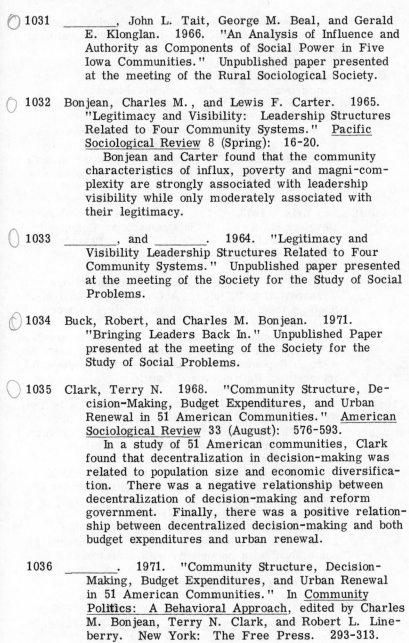

1031 _____, John L. Tait, George M. Beal, and Gerald E. Klonglan. 1966. "An Analysis of Influence and Authority as Components of Social Power in Five Iowa Communities." Unpublished paper presented at the meeting of the Rural Sociological Society.

1032 Bonjean, Charles M., and Lewis F. Carter. 1965. "Legitimacy and Visibility: Leadership Structures Related to Four Community Systems." Pacific Sociological Review 8 (Spring): 16-20.
    Bonjean and Carter found that the community characteristics of influx, poverty and magni-complexity are strongly associated with leadership visibility while only moderately associated with their legitimacy.

1033 _____, and _____. 1964. "Legitimacy and Visibility Leadership Structures Related to Four Community Systems." Unpublished paper presented at the meeting of the Society for the Study of Social Problems.

1034 Buck, Robert, and Charles M. Bonjean. 1971. "Bringing Leaders Back In." Unpublished Paper presented at the meeting of the Society for the Study of Social Problems.

1035 Clark, Terry N. 1968. "Community Structure, Decision-Making, Budget Expenditures, and Urban Renewal in 51 American Communities." American Sociological Review 33 (August): 576-593.
    In a study of 51 American communities, Clark found that decentralization in decision-making was related to population size and economic diversification. There was a negative relationship between decentralization of decision-making and reform government. Finally, there was a positive relationship between decentralized decision-making and both budget expenditures and urban renewal.

1036 _____. 1971. "Community Structure, Decision-Making, Budget Expenditures, and Urban Renewal in 51 American Communities." In Community Politics: A Behavioral Approach, edited by Charles M. Bonjean, Terry N. Clark, and Robert L. Lineberry. New York: The Free Press. 293-313.

1037 _____. 1969. "A Comparative Study of Community

Structures and Leadership." Unpublished paper
presented at the meeting of the American Political
Science Association.

1038 Clelland, Donald, and William Form. 1964. "Economic Dominants and Community Power: A Comparative Analysis." American Journal of Sociology
69 (March): 511-521.
    An absentee-owned corporation community was
examined and compared with an earlier study by
Robert Schulze. The results were similar in both
studies. A bifurcation of economic and political
interests had occurred.

1039 Cohen, Erik. 1973. "The Power Structure of Israeli
Development Towns." In Comparative Community
Politics, edited by Terry N. Clark. Beverly Hills,
Cal.: Sage Publications.

1040 Colcord, Frank C., Jr. 1968. "Decision-Making and
Transportation Policies: A Comparative Analysis."
Southwestern Social Science Quarterly 48 (December): 383-397.
    Despite changes in the community actors involved
in transportation decision-making, highway agencies
were still powerful and were supported by powerful
interests in Baltimore and Seattle.

1041 Conway, William J. 1970. "Power Structures in Two
Communities: A Comparative Analysis." Unpublished Ph.D. dissertation, Louisiana State University and Agricultural and Mechanical College.

1042 Crain, Robert L., and Donald B. Rosenthal. 1966.
"Structure and Values in Local Political Systems:
The Case of Fluoridation Decisions." Journal of
Politics 28 (February): 169-195.
    Crain and Rosenthal found that a favorable
fluoridation decision would have a better chance to
come about in a community with a centralized decision-making structure and with a low level of
direct citizen participation.

1043 _____, Elihu Katz, and Donald Rosenthal. 1969.
The Politics of Community Conflict: The Fluoridation Decision. Indianapolis: Bobbs-Merrill.

1044 Crenson, Matthew A. 1971. The Un-Politics of Air
      Pollution: A Study of Non-Decision Making in the
      Cities. Baltimore: Johns Hopkins Press.

1045 Dakin, Ralph E. 1962. "Variations in Power Struc-
      tures and Organizing Efficiency: A Comparative
      Study of Four Areas." Sociological Quarterly 3
      (July): 228-250.
          A comparison of the relationship between varia-
      tions in influence and potential power across issue
      areas.

1046 Daniels, Bruce C. 1970. "Large Town Power Struc-
      tures in Eighteenth Century Connecticut: An Analy-
      sis of Political Leadership in Hartford, Norwich,
      and Fairfield." Unpublished Ph. D. dissertation,
      University of Connecticut.

1047 D'Antonio, William. 1958. "National Images of Busi-
      ness and Political Elites in the Border Cities."
      Unpublished Ph. D. dissertation, Michigan State
      University.

1048 _____, and William H. Form. 1965. Influentials
      in Two Border Cities: A Study in Community De-
      cision-Making. South Bend, Ind. : University of
      Notre Dame Press.
          A comparison of decision-making and power in
      El Paso, Texas, and Ciudad Juarez, Mexico. The
      power structure was more concentrated at the top in
      Ciudad Juarez than El Paso because decision-
      making was more closely associated with formal
      authority there. While neither community had a
      monolithic power structure, major community de-
      cisions always involved only a few people. They
      did change by issue but still represented a small
      range of economic and political interests.

1049 _____, _____, Charles Loomis, and Eugene
      Erickson. 1961. "Institutional and Occupational
      Representatives in Eleven Community Influence
      Systems." American Sociological Review 26 (June):
      440-446.
          A comparison of the power structure data of
      D'Antonio et al. and the data of Delbert Miller.
      The data revealed that top businessmen were the

most highly represented group among the top and
big influentials. The model of general business
dominance was rejected.

1050   Davis, Morris, and Marvin Weinbaum. 1969. Metro-
       politan Decision Processes: An Analysis of Case
       Studies. Chicago: Rand McNally.

1051   Dodge, Lawrence Burnham. 1972. "A Human Ecolog-
       ical Approach to the Study of Power Distribution in
       Local Communities." Unpublished Ph. D. disserta-
       tion, Brown University.
          A comparative study of 51 American cities using
       two measures of power distribution; Amos Hawley's
       'MPO Ratio' and Terry Clark's 'IMS Index'. Dodge
       found that power concentration increases with power
       centralization and the more dominant (Hawley) a
       city the more concentrated and decentralized the
       power structure.

1052   Downes, Bryan T. 1968. "Suburban Differentiation
       and Municipal Policy Choices: A Comparative
       Analysis of Suburban Political Systems." In Com-
       munity Structure and Decision-Making: Compara-
       tive Analyses. San Francisco: Chandler Pub. Co.
       243-267.

1053   Duggan, Thomas Joseph. 1963. "Aldermanic Cam-
       paign Techniques and Decision-Making Systems in
       Two Communities." Unpublished Ph. D. disserta-
       tion, University of Illinois.

1054   Form, William, and William V. D'Antonio. 1959.
       "Integration and Cleavage Among Community In-
       fluentials in Two Border Cities." American Socio-
       logical Review 24 (December): 804-814.
          A study of integration patterns among community
       influentials in an American city and a Mexican city.
       It was found that integration was greater in the
       American city among its influentials.

1055   Fowler, Irving A. 1958. "Local Industry Structures,
       Economic Power, and Community Welfare." Social
       Problems 6 (Summer): 41-51.
          Fowler found that small-business cities did not
       have higher levels of welfare than big-business
       cities. The type of local industry was an important

criterion in deciding welfare levels. Fowler concluded that 'concentrations of economic power' did not show any adverse effects on community welfare.

1056 _____. 1964. Local Industrial Structures, Economic Power, and Community Welfare: Thirty Small New York State Cities 1930-1950. Totowa, N. J.: Bedminster Press.

1057 Fox, Douglas M. 1972. "Ideology and Community Politics: Two Case Studies." Polity 4 (Spring): 367-374.
   Fox tested the concept of ideology originally posited by Agger, Goldrich, and Swanson (in The Rulers and the Ruled). They argued that ideology was important in understanding local political behavior. Fox could not validate their argument and concluded that their findings on ideology did not help to understand community leadership in the communities that he examined.

1058 _____. 1968. "Power Structure in Two Suburban Communities: Montville and Waterford, Connecticut." Unpublished Ph.D. dissertation, Columbia University.

1059 Fried, Robert C. 1973. "Politics, Economics, and Federalism: Aspects of Urban Government in Mittel-Europa." In Comparative Community Politics, edited by Terry N. Clark. Beverly Hills, Cal.: Sage Publications.

1060 Froman, Lewis A., Jr. 1967. "An Analysis of Public Policies in Cities." Journal of Politics 29 (February): 94-108.
   A typology for studying policy categories was developed. Froman argues that policies should be studied on two levels: area policies which tend to be associated with homogeneous communities, and segmental policies which tend to be associated with heterogeneous communities.

1061 Goldrich, Daniel. 1959. "Parties, Partisanship and Local Politics in Two Oregon Communities." Unpublished Ph.D. dissertation, University of North Carolina.

1062   Greco, Giacchino. 1970. "Potere e Parentela nella
        Sicilia Nuova" [Power and Kinship in the New
        Sicily]. Quaderni di Sociologia 19 (Jan.-Mar.):
        3-41.
            Kinship was not found to carry much political
        weight in six Sicilian villages.

1063   Grimes, Michael D., J. Larry Lyon, and Charles M.
        Bonjean. 1973. "Community Structure and Leader-
        ship Structure: A Comparative Analysis of 39 Com-
        munities." Unpublished paper presented at the
        meeting of the American Sociological Association.

1064   Hanna, W. J., and J. L. Hanna. 1969. "Influence
        and Influentials in Two Urban-Centered African
        Communities." Comparative Politics 2 (October):
        17-40.
            The attainment of influence in these communities
        was based on ascriptive characteristics and service
        to certain ethnic groups.

1065   Horton, John E., and Wayne E. Thompson. 1962.
        "Powerlessness and Political Negativism: A Study
        of Defeated Local Referendums." American Jour-
        nal of Sociology 67 (March): 485-493.
            Powerless groups used negative voting behavior
        in local referenda as an outlet for protest. The
        protests were not class-conscious opposition but a
        convergence of all the powerless groups as a mass
        protest.

1066   Jacob, Phillip E. 1971. "Leaders' Values and the
        Dynamics of Community Integration: A Four-Nation
        Comparative Study." In Community Politics: A
        Behavioral Approach, edited by Charles M. Bonjean,
        Terry N. Clark, and Robert L. Lineberry. New
        York: The Free Press. 250-262.
            Community leaders' values were strikingly dif-
        ferent in different national contexts. This brief
        report on a major study of community leaders in
        Yugoslavia, Poland, India, and the U.S. summarizes
        some of the major cross-national differences. Dif-
        ferences across countries in resource mobilization
        and involvement in community affairs were also pre-
        sented.

1067   _____. 1967. "Projekt Porownawczych Badan nad

Wartosciami i Decyzjami Ludzi Wladzy Lokalnej"
[A Comparative Research Project Concerning Values
and Decisions of Local Leaders]. Studia Socjologiczno Polityczne 23: 143-158.

1068 _____, Henry Teune, and Thomas Watts. 1968.
"Values, Leadership and Development: A Four
Nation Study. " Social Science Information 7 (April):
49-92.

1069 Jambrek, Peter. 1973. "Socio-Economic Change and
Political Development: Decision-Making in 16 Yugoslav Communes. " In Comparative Community Politics, edited by Terry N. Clark. Beverly Hills,
Cal. : Sage Publications.

1070 _____. 1971. "Socio-Economic Development and
Political Change in Yugoslav Communes. " Unpublished Ph. D. dissertation, University of Chicago.

1071 Johnston, Ray E. 1967. "A Comparative Analysis of
Demand Articulation in Three Western Communities. "
Unpublished Ph. D. dissertation, University of Ore-
gon.

1072 Kammerer, Gladys M. , Charles Farris, John DeGrove,
Alfred Clubok. 1963. The Urban Political Community: Profiles in Town Politics. Boston:
Houghton Mifflin.
    Manager tenure and turnover was determined by
power exchanges in the communities studied. The
tenure of the manager was longer in communities
with monopolistic power structures. Also, it was
found that elected mayors posed a threat to city
managers.

1073 Kammeyer, Kenneth. 1963. "Community Homogeneity
and Decision-Making. " Rural Sociology 20 (September): 238-245.
    In a study of 110 small communities, Kammeyer
found that ethnically homogeneous communities dis-
played less opposition to the loss of their high
schools than did heterogeneous communities. Kammeyer argues that this finding is a reflection of the
greater integration in homogeneous communities.

1074 Keeler, John B. , and Courtney B. Clelland. 1971.

"Community Power Research in Four Villages of
Sonora, Mexico." Unpublished paper presented at
the meeting of the American Sociological Association.

1075 Kesselman, Mark. 1973. "Linkages Between Party
Activists and Local Public Officials in France."
In Comparative Community Politics, edited by
Terry N. Clark. Beverly Hills, Cal.: Sage Pub-
lications.

1076 _____. 1970. "Overinstitutionalization and Political
Constraint: The Case of France." Comparative
Politics 3 (October): 21-44.
A study of the relationship between local govern-
ment and local notables with the national govern-
ment of France.

1077 Kurtz, James Stanley. 1971. "A Paradigm for Power
Structure Research." Unpublished Ed. D. dissertation, University of Nebraska.

1078 LaFontaine, Edward D. 1971. "The Dynamics of
Power and Decision-Making in Two Small Commu-
nities." Unpublished master's thesis, Ohio State
University.

1079 Lakshminarayana, H. D. 1970. "Dominant Caste and
Power Structure." Behavioral Sciences & Community Development 4 (September): 146-160.

1080 Larsen, Calvin J. 1965. "Economic and Ecological
Factors in Relation to Community Leadership Structure: A Comparative and Historical Analysis of
Two Oregon Communities. Unpublished Ph. D. dissertation, University of Oregon.

1081 Lyons, Schley R. 1964. "City Councils and County
Boards in Action: A Comparative Study of Suburban
Decision-Making." Unpublished Ph. D. dissertation,
The American University.

1082 McFatter, William T., Jr. 1970. "The Degree,
Level, Pattern, and Efficacy of Citizen Participation in Policy Matters Under Different Types of
Community Power Structure." Unpublished Ed. D.
dissertation, University of Florida.

1083   Mayer, Peter B.   1971.   "Moffussil: Political Change
       and Community Politics in Two Indian Provincial
       Cities." Unpublished Ph. D. dissertation, Univer-
       sity of Wisconsin.

1084   Michel, Jerry B.   1964.   "The Measurement of Social
       Power on the Community Level: An Exploratory
       Study." American Journal of Economics and So-
       ciology 23 (April): 189-196.
           Michel found that business elites in metropolitan
       areas do not have the same degree of control in
       their communities as business elites in small com-
       munities. Michel used municipal tax rates as the
       key index of social power.

1085   _____.   1962.   "The Measurement of Social Power
       on the Community Level: An Exploratory Study."
       Unpublished paper presented at the meeting of the
       Southwestern Sociological Society.

1086   Miller, Delbert C.   1958.   "Decision-Making Cliques
       in Community Power Structures: A Comparative
       Study of an American and an English City." Amer-
       ican Journal of Sociology 54 (November): 299-309.
           Miller found that the pyramidal structure of
       power was not appropriate in the two communities
       that he studied. Instead, he proposed a ring or
       cone model with influence and power flowing out
       from the center.

1087   _____.   1958.   "Industry and Community Power
       Structure: A Comparative Study of an American
       and an English City. American Sociological Re-
       view 23 (February): 9-15.
           The hypothesis that businessmen exert predomi-
       nant influence in community decision-making was
       supported in the American city but not in the Eng-
       lish city. Miller argues that this was due to the
       different power structures as related to city coun-
       cils in each city as well as the different occupa-
       tional prestige systems in each city.

1088   _____.   1970.   International Community Power
       Structures. Bloomington: Indiana University Press.
           A comparison of the power structures of Seattle,
       Bristol, Cordoba, and Lima. The major similarity
       among the power structures of the four cities was

reliance of the cities on the business sector. The
major difference was the military influence in the
power structures of Lima and Cordoba.

1089 Morlock, Laura L. 1971. "Business Interests,
Countervailing Groups and the Balance of Influence
in 91 Cities. Unpublished paper presented at the
meeting of the Society for the Study of Social Problems.

1090 Moser, Ruth. 1967. "Correlates of Decision-Making
in Eighteen New England Communities." Unpublished M.A. thesis, University of Chicago.

1091 Newton, Kenneth. 1969. "City Politics in Britain and
the United States." Political Studies 17 (June):
208-218.

1092 _____. 1973. "Community Decision-Makers and
Community Decision-Making in England and the
United States." In Comparative Community Poli-
tics, edited by Terry N. Clark. Beverly Hills,
Cal.: Sage Publications.

1093 _____. 1970. "Community Decision-Making and
Community Decision-Makers in England and the
United States." Unpublished paper presented at
the meeting of the International Sociological Association.

1094 Preston, James D., and Danette Spiekerman. 1969.
"The Relationship Between Community Characteristics and Power Structure Characteristics: An
Examination of Smaller Communities." Unpublished
paper presented at the meeting of the Rural Sociological Society.

1095 _____, _____, and Patricia B. Guseman. 1972.
"The Identification of Leadership in Two Texas
Communities: A Replication of the Bonjean Technique." Sociological Quarterly 13 (Fall): 508-
515.

1096 Pusic, Eugen. 1973. "Diversity and Integration in
the Yugoslav Commune. In Comparative Community
Politics, edited by Terry N. Clark: Beverly Hills,
Cal.: Sage Publications.

1097   Rhyne, Edwin Hoffman.   1958.   "Political Parties and
       Decision-Making in Three Southern Counties."
       American Political Science Review 52 (December):
       1091-1107.

1098   Roig, Charles, Christian Mingasson, and Pierre
       Kukawka.   1970.   "Social Structure and Local
       Power Structure in Urban Areas.   Analysis of
       17 French Townships."   The New Atlantis 1
       (Winter):   65-84.

1099   Rosenthal, Donald B.   1966.   "Administrative Politics
       in Two Indian Cities."   Asian Survey 6 (April):
       201-215.

1100   _____.   1966.   "Deference and Friendship Patterns
       in Two Indian Municipal Councils."   Social Forces
       45 (December):   178-192.

1101   _____.   1966.   "Factions and Alliances in Indian
       City Politics."   Midwest Journal of Political
       Science 10 (August):   320-349.
           Rosenthal argues that factions are important in
       building alliances in Indian politics.   The strengths
       and weaknesses of the alliances can be traced to
       the characteristics of the factions themselves.

1102   _____.   1968.   "Functions of Urban Political Sys-
       tems: Comparative Analysis and the Indian Case."
       In Community Structure and Decision-Making:
       Comparative Analyses, edited by Terry N. Clark.
       San Francisco: Chandler Pub. Co.   269-303.

1103   _____.   1970.   The Limited Elite: Politics and
       Government in Two Indian Cities.   Chicago: Uni-
       versity of Chicago Press.

1104   _____.   1964.   "The Politics of Community Con-
       flict."   Unpublished Ph.D. dissertation, University
       of Chicago.

1105   _____, and Robert L. Crain.   1968.   "Structure
       and Values in Local Political Systems: The Case
       of Fluoridation Decisions."   In Community Structure
       and Decision-Making: Comparative Analyses, edited
       by Terry N. Clark.   San Francisco: Chandler
       Pub. Co.   215-242.

1106   Sastrodiningrat, Soebagio.   1964.   "Some Dimensions
       of Power and Influence in Relation to the Power
       Structure Data in Two Cities."   Unpublished Ph. D.
       dissertation, Indiana University.

1107   Schultze, William A.   1967.   "Public Leadership in
       Charter Revision: Case Studies in Four New Jersey
       Municipalities."   Unpublished Ph. D. dissertation,
       Rutgers University.

1108   Shields, William Anthony.   1972.   "Power Structures
       of Four Idaho Communities: A Test of an Alterna-
       tive Methodology."   Unpublished Ph. D. dissertation,
       University of Pittsburgh.

1109   Singh, Avtar.   1967.   "Leadership Patterns and Village
       Structure: A Study of Six Indian Villages."   Un-
       published Ph. D. dissertation, Mississippi State Uni-
       versity.

1110   Stevens, Jimmie W.   1967.   "Community Influentials:
       A Comparative Study of Two Florida Counties."
       Unpublished Ph. D. dissertation, Florida State Uni-
       versity.

1111   Sutton, Willis A., Jr.   1969.   "Perceptions of Power:
       Comparisons of Leader and Random Sample Reputa-
       tion Rosters in an Eastern Kentucky County and in
       Burlington, N. C. --A Replication of Bonjean's Con-
       cealed, Visible, and Symbolic Leader Analysis."
       Unpublished paper presented at the meeting of the
       Southern Sociological Society.

1112   Tait, John L.   1970.   "Power Structure by Issue Area
       in Five Iowa Communities."   Unpublished Ph. D.
       dissertation, Iowa State University.

1113   _____, and George M. Beal.   1965.   "An Analysis
       of Power Structures in Five Iowa Towns."   Unpub-
       lished paper presented at the meeting of the Rural
       Sociological Society.

1114   Walsh, Annmarie Hauck.   1969.   The Urban Challenge
       to Government.   New York: Praeger.

1115   Walter, Benjamin.   1960.   "Political Decision-Making
       in North Carolina Cities."   PROD 3 (May):   18-21.

1116 Walton, John. 1970. "Development Decision Making:
      A Comparative Study in Latin America." American
      Journal of Sociology 75 (March): 828-851.

1117 Weingrod, Alex. 1971. "Immigrants, Localism, and
      Political Power: An American-Israel Comparison."
      International Journal of Politics 1 (Spring): 90-103.

1118 Weirath, T. J. 1966. "Mayoral Recruitment in Four
      Wisconsin Cities: An Investigation into Historical
      Sociology." Unpublished master's thesis, Univer-
      sity of Wisconsin.

1119 Wenger, Dennis E. 1970. "Toward a Comparative
      Model for the Analysis of Community Power: A
      Conceptualization and Empirical Application." Un-
      published Ph.D. dissertation, Ohio State University.

1120 Werlin, Herbert H. 1966. "The Nairobi City Coun-
      cil: A Study in Comparative Local Government."
      Comparative Studies in Society and History 7
      (January): 181-198.

1121 Westerstahl, Jorgen. 1973. "Decision-Making Sys-
      tems in 36 Swedish Communes." In Comparative
      Community Politics, edited by Terry N. Clark.
      Beverly Hills, Cal.: Sage Publications.

1122 _____. 1970. "Decision-Making Systems in 36
      Swedish Communes: A Research Report." Un-
      published paper presented at the meeting of the
      American Political Science Association.

1123 Whitten, Norman E., Jr. 1965. "Power Structure
      and Sociocultural Change in Latin American Com-
      munities." Social Forces 43 (March): 320-329.
          A comparative study of 19 communities found
      that as the local power structure loses its depen-
      dence on local religion, the communities start to
      assume the national cultural orientation. From
      this, the power structure assumes a greater auton-
      omy.

1124 Wiley, Norbert Francis. 1962. "Class and Local
      Politics in Three Michigan Communities." Unpub-
      lished Ph.D. dissertation, Michigan State Univer-
      sity.

1125 Williams, Oliver P. , and Charles R. Adrian. 1963.
      Four Cities: A Study in Comparative Policy Making.
      Philadelphia: University of Pennsylvania Press.
          Williams and Adrian found that the policies con-
      cerning economic growth drew wide support from
      higher income groups and opposition from lower
      income groups. Conversely, lower income groups
      favored caretaker government.

1126 Wood, Robert C. 1961. 1400 Governments. Cam-
      bridge, Mass. : Harvard University Press.
          Wood found that the governments he studied left
      the important decisions concerning regional develop-
      ment to the private marketplace. A factor analysis
      of municipal finance was also presented, using the
      data from cities in the greater New York area.

5

STUDY OF COMMUNITY POWER AND DECISION-MAKING

AS A FIELD OF RESEARCH

1127 Bell, Colin, and Howard Newby. 1972. Community
Studies: An Introduction to the Sociology of the
Local Community. New York: Praeger.

1128 Clark, Terry N. 1970. "Introduction to the Issue:
Current Topics in Research on Community Decision-Making." The New Atlantis 1 (Winter):
3-11.

1129 _____. 1968. "Present and Future Research on
Community Decision-Making: The Problems of
Comparability." In Community Structure and De-
cision-Making: Comparative Analyses, edited by
Terry N. Clark. San Francisco: Chandler Pub.
Co. 463-478.

1130 Dahl, Robert. 1959. "Business and Politics: A
Critical Appraisal of Political Science." American
Political Science Review 53 (March): 1-34.

1131 Daland, Robert T. 1957. "Political Science and the
Study of Urbanism." American Political Science
Review 51 (June): 491-509.

1132 Danzger, M. Herbert. 1964. "Community Power
Structure: Problems and Continuities." American
Sociological Review 29 (October): 707-717.

1133 Dye, Thomas R. 1969-70. "Community Power
Studies." Political Science Annual 2: 35-70.

1134 _____, editor. 1966. Comparative Research in
Community Politics. Athens, Ga.: Proceedings
of the Conference on Comparative Research in Community Politics.

1135   Ferraresi, France.   1971.   Studi sul Potere Locale:
       Materiali per l'Aralisi delle Strutture di Potere
       nelle Comunità Locali, con Particolare Riferimento
       agli Studi Classici Americani [Studies of Local
       Power: Material for the Analysis of the Structure
       of Power in Local Communities with Particular
       Reference to Classical American Studies].   Milan:
       Giuffre.

1136   Fisher, Sethard.   1962.   "Community Power Studies:
       A Critique."   Social Research 29 (Winter):   449-
       466.

1137   Fox, Douglas M.   1971.   "Whither Community Power
       Studies."   Polity 3 (September):   576-585.

1138   Friedmann, Peter.   1970.   "Community Decision-Making
       in the United States: A Review of Recent Re-
       search."   The New Atlantis 1 (Winter):   133-142.
       A review of recent research with an emphasis
       on the effect of this research on substantive issue
       areas presently being debated by researchers.
       Comparative studies are stressed, as are studies
       relating leadership and power to different patterns
       of policy outputs.

1139   Gourney, B.   1963.   "L'Etude des Décisions Politiques:
       Note Introductive" [The Study of Political Decision-
       Making: Introductory Note].   Revue Française de
       Science Politique 13 (Juin):   348-352.

1140   Herson, Lawrence J. R.   1961.   "In the Footsteps of
       Community Power."   American Political Science
       Review 55 (December):   817-830.
       A review and critique of community power
       studies, especially the work of Floyd Hunter.

1141   Hunter, Floyd.   1971.   "The Application of Computers
       to Community Power Study."   In Future Directions
       in Community Power Research: A Colloquium,
       edited by Frederick Wirt.   Berkeley: Institute for
       Governmental Studies, University of California,
       Berkeley.   96-104.

1142   Jacob, Herbert, and Michael Lipsky.   1968.   "Outputs,
       Structure, and Power on Assessment of Changes
       in the Study of State and Local Politics."   Journal

of Politics 30 (May):   510-538.
A review of the literature on state and local
politics over a twenty-year period.

1143   Janowitz, Morris.   1962.   "Community Power and
'Policy Science' Research."   Public Opinion
Quarterly 26 (Fall): 398-410.

1144   Leif, Irving P. , and Terry Nichols Clark.   1974.
Community Power and Decision-Making: A Trend
Report and Bibliography.   The Hague, Netherlands: Mouton for the Current Sociology Series
of UNESCO and the International Sociological Association.

1145   Long, Norton E.   1967.   "Political Science and the
City. "   In Urban Research and Policy Planning,
edited by Leo F. Schnore and Henry Fagin.
Beverly Hills, Cal. : Sage Publications.   243-262.

1146   _____, and George Belknap.   1956.   A Research
Program on Leadership and Decision-Making in
Metropolitan Areas.   New York: Governmental
Affairs Institute.

1147   Narojek, Winicjusz.   1964.   "Z Problematyki Americ-
kanskich Badan nad Wladza Lokalna" [Remarks on
American Research in Local Government].   Studia
Socjologiczno Polityczne 16: 95-106.
A review of previous American research on community decision-making found that the two most
used techniques, the reputational and the decisional,
contradict one another.   This indicated that each of
them was studying a different problem.   No comparative research using the same techniques over
a number of communities has been attempted as
yet.

1148   Rabinovitz, Francine.   1968.   "Sound and Fury Signi-
fying Nothing? A Review of Community Power Research in Latin America. "   Urban Affairs Quarterly
3 (March): 111-122.
After reviewing prior research on community
power in Latin America, Rabinovitz suggests that
more attention should be given to identifying the
different types of power structures and the instruments used to identify them.   An important guide.

1149 Rossi, Peter. 1957. "Community Decision-Making."
      Administrative Science Quarterly 1 (March): 415-
      443.
          An important review of research on community
      decision-making up to 1956. A critique of three
      approaches used to study decision-making up to that
      time; the decision-making approach, the 'partisan'
      approach, and the issue career approach.

1150 Sayre, Wallace S., and Nelson W. Polsby. 1965.
      "American Political Science and the Study of Ur-
      banization." In The Study of Urbanization, edited
      by Phillip Hauser and Leo F. Schnore. New York:
      John Wiley & Sons. 115-156.

1151 Schmid, Catherine. 1965. "Quelques Recherches
      Récentes sur le Problem du Pouvoir dans les
      Communautés Locales" [Some Recent Research on
      the Problem of Power in Local Communities].
      Sociologie du Travail 7 (April-June): 190-196.
          Schmid reviews the research by American and
      French sociologists who have employed the reputa-
      tional and decisional techniques. She concluded
      that both these techniques overlooked the mecha-
      nisms and nature of power. Schmid suggests the
      use of game theory in future power structure re-
      search.

1152 Stacey, Margaret. 1969. "The Myth of Community
      Studies." British Journal of Sociology 20 (June):
      134-147.

1153 Tabek, F. 1971. "Estudos de Politica Local--A
      Experiencia do Brasil" [Studies on Local Politics:
      Brazil's Experience]. Revista de Ciencia Politica
      5 (Avril-Juin): 61-90.

1154 Tarkowski, Jacek. 1967. "Aktywnosc Spolecznosci
      Lokalnej" [Activeness of Local Community Research
      Proposals]. Studia Socjologiczno Polityczne 23:
      165-175.

1155 Truman, David B. 1961. "Theory and Research on
      Metropolitan Political Leadership: Report on a
      Conference." Items 15 (March): 1-3.

1156 Tucker, W. P. 1969. "Latin American Local

Government: Trends in Study and Research."
Rocky Mountain Social Science Journal 6 (April):
182-188.

1157   Walton, John. 1973. "The Bearing of Social Science
Research on Public Issues: Floyd Hunter and the
Study of Power." In Cities in Change: Studies in
the Urban Condition, edited by John Walton and
Donald E. Carns. Boston: Allyn and Bacon. 318-
332.

1158   _____. 1971. "Why Study Power Structures? A
Critique and a Theoretical Proposal." In Future
Directions in Community Power Research: A
Colloquium, edited by Frederick Wirt. Berkeley:
Institute for Governmental Studies, University of
California, Berkeley. 147-166.

1159   Westerstahl, Jorgen. 1970. "The Communal Research
Program in Sweden." The New Atlantis 1 (Winter):
124-132.

1160   Wiatr, Jerzy J. 1967. "Wstep" [Introduction].
Studia Socjologiczne Polityczne 23: 7-11.

1161   Wirt, Frederick M. , editor. 1971. Future Directions in Community Power Research: A Colloquium.
Berkeley: Institute for Governmental Studies, University of California, Berkeley.

1162   Wood, Robert C. 1963. "The Contributions of Polit-
ical Science to Urban Form." In Urban Life and
Form, edited by Werner Z. Hirsch. New York:
Holt, Rinehart, & Winston. 99-127.

1163   Zawadski, Sylvester. 1970. "Study of Local Power in
Poland." Unpublished paper presented at the meeting of the International Political Science Association.

AND THE SOCIOLOGY OF KNOWLEDGE

1164   Adrian, Charles R. 1971. "Several Loose Ends in
Theory Building." In Future Directions in Com-
munity Power Research: A Colloquium, edited by
Frederick Wirt. Berkeley: Institute for

Governmental Studies, University of California, Berkeley.   3-5.

1165   Bonjean, Charles M. , and David Olson.   1964.   "Community Leadership: Directions of Research."   Administrative Science Quarterly 9 (December): 278-300.
A review of community studies was undertaken. Bonjean and Olson found a trend toward the use of the reputational and decisional techniques rather than the positional technique, leadership structures vary over time and place, and a trend away from case studies to comparative analysis.

1166   Brown, Theresa, M. J. C. Vile, and M. F. Whitmore. 1972.   "Community Studies and Decision-Making." British Journal of Political Science 2 (April):   133-153.

1167   Clark, Terry N. , William Kornblum, H. Bloom, and S. Tobias.   1968.   "Discipline, Method, Community Structure, and Decision-Making: The Role and Limitations of the Sociology of Knowledge." The American Sociologist 3 (August): 214-217.

1168   Curtis, James E. , and John W. Petras.   1970.   "Community Power, Power Studies, and the Sociology of Knowledge."   Human Organization 29 (Fall):   204-218.

1169   Gilbert, Claire W.   1971.   "Communities, Power Structures & Research Bias."   Polity 4 (Winter): 218-235.

1170   _____.   1968.   "Community Power and Decision-Making: A Quantitative Examination of Previous Research."   In Community Structure and Decision-Making: Comparative Analyses, edited by Terry N. Clark. San Francisco: Chandler Pub. Co. 139-156.

1171   _____.   1972.   Community Power Structure: Propositional Inventory, Tests, and Theory. Gainesville: Social Sciences Research Monograph #45, University of Florida Press.

1172   _____.   1966.   "Community Power Structure: A

Study in the Sociology of Knowledge." Unpublished
Ph.D. dissertation, Northwestern University.

1173 _____. 1965. "Community Power Studies: Why
the Difference in Findings." Unpublished M.A.
thesis, Northwestern University.

1174 _____. 1967. "Some Trends in Community Politics: A Secondary Analysis of Power Structure
Data From 166 Communities." Southwestern Social
Science Quarterly 48 (December): 373-381.
    A secondary analysis of community power studies
from 1929 through 1964. The purpose of the study
was to pinpoint trends in community politics and to
try to find any differences in research findings between sociologists and political scientists.

1175 _____. 1968. "The Study of Community Power:
A Summary and a Test." In The New Urbaniza-
tion, edited by Scott Greer and David Minar. New
York: St. Martin's Press. 222-245.

1176 Hildahl, Spencer H. 1970. "A Note on '... a Note
on the Sociology of Knowledge'." Sociological
Quarterly 11 (Summer): 405-415.

1177 Institute of Public Administration, University of the
Philippines. 1959. "Research Findings on Problems of Local Government." Philippine Journal
of Public Administration 3 (January): 11-15.

1178 Kellstedt, Lyman. 1965. "Atlanta to 'Oretown'--
Identifying Community Elites." Public Administration Review 25 (June): 161-168.

1179 Nelson, Michael Davidson. 1972. "Community Power
Structure: Fact or Artifact?" Unpublished M.A.
thesis, Carleton University.

1180 Polsby, Nelson. 1963. Community Power and Political Theory. New Haven, Conn.: Yale University
Press.
    A critique of the methods and findings of the
major studies of community power and decision-
making by Hunter, Schulze, Pellegrin and Coates,
Baltzell, the Lynds, Warner, Hollingshead, and
Miller. Polsby also calls for research on specific

community decisions rather than the study of power
by the reputational technique.

1181   Richards, Allan R.   1954.   "Local Government Re-
       search: A Partial Evaluation."   Public Adminis-
       tration Review 14 (Autumn): 271-277.

1182   Shepard, Morris A.   1969.   "Community Power Struc-
       tures: A Typology and Societal Correlates."   Un-
       published Ph. D. dissertation, University of Connec-
       ticut.
           A secondary analysis of 24 community power
       studies.   A typology of five basic types of commu-
       nity power structures and societal correlates were
       developed from this analysis.

1183   Sjoberg, Gideon.   1955.   "Urban Community Theory
       and Research: A Partial Evaluation."   American
       Journal of Economics and Sociology 14 (January):
       199-206.

1184   Vidich, Arthur, Joseph Bensman, and Maurice Stein.
       1964.   Reflections on Community Studies.   New
       York: John Wiley & Sons.

1185   Walton, John T.   1966.   "An Analysis of Methods and
       Findings in Studies of Community Power Structure."
       Unpublished Ph. D. dissertation, University of Cali-
       fornia, Santa Barbara.

1186   _____.   1966.   "Discipline, Method and Community
       Power: A Note on the Sociology of Knowledge."
       American Sociological Review 31 (October):   684-
       689.
           A comparison of the results of community power
       studies by sociologists and political scientists re-
       veals that the disciplinary background of an investi-
       gator has a tendency to determine the method of
       investigation which, in turn, tends to determine the
       power structure that will be found.   Walton argues
       that the use of a combination of research methods
       would be a protection against this bias.

1187   _____.   1966.   "Substance and Artifact: The Cur-
       rent Status of Research on Community Power Struc-
       ture."   American Journal of Sociology 71 (January):
       430-438.

Walton found that when a single research technique was used, the type of power structure found
may have been an artifact of that method.   Other
variables that show an effect on the power structure are social integration, region, and industrialization.   The use of a comparative technique was
recommended.

1188 _____. 1970. "A Systematic Survey of Community
Power Research." In The Structure of Community
Power, edited by Michael Aiken and Paul Mott.
New York: Random House. 443-464.

1189 Yoshihashi, Sumiko. 1968. "A Critique of the Study
Made About Community Power Structure--Its Prob-
lems, Methods and Views in the United States."
Shakaigaku Hyoron 18 (March): 14-32.

BIBLIOGRAPHIES OF RESEARCH

1190 Cazzola, Franco. 1971. "Bibliografia" [Bibliography].
Scienze Sociali 1 (April): 124-144.

1191 Gore, William J., and Fred S. Silander. 1959. "A
Bibliographical Essay on Decision-Making." Administrative Science Quarterly 4 (June): 97-121.

1192 Hawley, Willis D., and James H. Svara. 1972. The
Study of Community Power: A Bibliographic Review. Santa Barbara, Cal.: American Bibliographic Center--Clio Press, Inc.

1193 Morlan, Robert L. 1965. "Foreign Local Government: A Bibliography." American Political
Science Review 59 (March): 120-137.

1194 Pellegrin, Roland J. 1967. "Selected Bibliography on
Community Power Structure." Southwestern Social
Science Quarterly 48 (December): 451-465.

1195 Press, Charles. 1962. Main Street Politics: Policy
Making at the Local Level. East Lansing: Institute
for Community Development, Michigan State University.

1196 Wasserman, Paul, and Fred S. Silander. 1958. De-
      cision Making: An Annotated Bibliography. Ithaca,
      N. Y. : Graduate School of Business and Public Ad-
      ministration, Cornell University.

AUTHOR INDEX

Abbott, A. P. 890
Aberbach, J. D. 744
Abramson, E. 1
Abu-Laban, B. 367, 508,
  712-715
Acker, R. D. 716
Adrian, C. R. 153, 329,
  414-416, 528, 529, 717,
  718, 1015, 1017, 1125,
  1164
Agger, R. 2, 184, 185,
  212, 213, 321, 509, 812,
  1018, 1019
Agulla, J. C. 641
Aiken, M. 214, 417, 564,
  863, 864, 990, 1020,
  1021
Akenson, C. B. 865
Akimoto, R. 186, 510, 719
Akpan, E. E. 215
Alford, R. R. 154, 187,
  188, 216, 863, 864, 990,
  991, 1021-1023
Allcock, J. B. 930
Allegrucci, R. L. 1024
Allen, C. H. 511
Alred, C. E. 970
Altshuler, A. A. 891
Amendola, G. 418
American Academy of Polit-
  ical and Social Science
  419
Anderson, T. A. 811
Anderson, W. 420, 421
Andrews, W. D. 966
Angell, R. C. 422
Anton, T. 3, 4, 1025
Arensburg, C. C. 322

Ashley, T. J. 866
Ashraf, A. 512
Auerbach, A. J. 513, 867

Babchuck, N. 720
Bachrach, P. 5, 6, 155,
  156, 940, 941
Bailey, N. A. 514
Balbo, L. 423, 515
Baltzell, E. D. 516
Banfield, E. C. 114, 217,
  517, 721, 880, 1026
Banwell, H. 218
Baratz, M. 6, 155, 156
Bard, A. A. de 219
Barkley, R. 7
Barlow, H. M. 518
Barth, E. A. T. 424,
  892, 1027, 1028
Bartholomew, D. K. 519
Bassett, R. E. 323
Bates, R. L. 240
Bauer, M. L. 924
Bauman, Z. 8, 324
Beal, G. M. 143, 723,
  813, 967, 969, 1030,
  1031, 1113
Beck, C. 325
Belknap, G. M. 520, 799,
  913, 1146
Belknap, I. 951
Bell, C. 1127
Bell, W. 115
Bellush, J. 868, 893
Bensman, J. 9, 697, 968,
  1184
Berger, S. 722

159